BIBLE BYTES for Teens

A Study-Devotional for Logging In to God's Word

P.O. Box 4123 Lancaster, PA 17604
www.starburstpublishers.com

Visit www.starburstpublishers.com

CREDITS:
Written by Alison J. Hutchins
Edited by Chad Allen
Cover design by Richmond & Williams
Text design and composition by Booksetters

Starburst Publishers, P.O. Box 4123, Lancaster, PA 17604

First printing, May 2001
ISBN: 1-892016-49-4
Library of Congress Catalog Number: 00-193614
Printed in USA

Contents

Introduction

Wouldn't it be great if God had a home page? Any time you wanted to plug in to God's thoughts, you could simply select the "God" icon and (click!) God's site would pop up, complete with eye-dazzling effects and digitized tunes. Then you could choose from links like "Here's what I have to say about dating" and "Want to know what I think of *you*? Click here."

In many ways God's home page already exists, and has for hundreds of years, within the pages of Scripture. The Bible is where you can log in to God's wisdom. Sometimes the Bible's message is sweet. Sometimes it pierces you to the core. But one thing is certain—the Bible is your gateway to a life of total fulfillment.

God created you, so he alone knows what will satisfy your inner longings. Tap into that satisfaction by working to see through the glitzy promises of sin, which are always lies, and grab hold of truth, which is God's Word.

Bible Bytes for Teens is a fast way to go extreme into Scripture. Each study opens with a short story about teens like you who grapple with hard issues. In the sidebar you'll find the heart of this book—a quote from the Bible under "Download Bible Byte." Next you'll start "processing" the Bible and exploring its wisdom for your life. Then you'll lock what you learn into your memory banks by answering a few questions. Finally, don't forget to read the study's "highlight."

This book is organized into five sections that take you from your relationship with God to your personal life to your relationships with others. It doesn't matter whether you go from the first study to the last or skip around, but each study has a unique message, so don't miss any of them!

Reading the Bible is one of the best things you can do for yourself. The more you fill your mind with truth, the more you'll be able to tell right from wrong and make wise decisions. Happy surfing!

Chad Allen
Editor

Committed to God

Committed to God
Committed to God

Faith Versus Fear

"Come on, Kim! Let yourself fall!"

"Yeah! We'll catch you!"

Kim clenched her fists at her sides and glanced at the ground five feet below. It was her first day at summer camp, and her counselor was making her conquer the trust fall. She had to stand on the platform with her back to the members of her group and fall into their waiting arms.

"I can't do this," she said, but her words were drowned out by her group's shouts of encouragement. Soon they were chanting her name, and Kim knew she'd have to go through with it. But the thought of letting herself plummet backwards was terrifying. There were at least ten people waiting below, but what if she slipped through their arms onto the hard ground?

"What are you afraid of, Kim?" the counselor yelled. "Don't you trust us?"

DOWNLOAD BIBLE BYTE

Without warning, a furious storm came up on the lake, so that the waves swept over the boat. But Jesus was sleeping. The disciples went and woke him, saying, "Lord, save us! We're going to drown!" He replied, "You of little faith, why are you so afraid?"
Matthew 8:24–26

Processing

The disciples believed that Jesus, because he was God's Son, had the power to save them from drowning. They just didn't have enough faith to wait out the storm. Jesus rebuked the disciples because they gave in to fear, and their fear showed that they lacked faith in Jesus' control.

When life's storms hit, it's easy to act just like the disciples, forgetting that God is in control. Even if we believe he has the power to take care of us, we might think he's unaware of the danger we're in.

Kim was fearful for the same reason all of us get fearful—she lacked faith. Kim didn't trust her group even though they promised not to drop her. Despite their good intentions, she knew the group could make a mistake and let her fall.

Trusting God isn't like trusting people. When we place our faith in God, we can rest assured he'll never drop us. Unlike Kim's group members, God is perfect in every way—power, knowledge, wisdom, and love. He never closes his eyes, looks away, or even blinks. In Isaiah 49:15–16 God tells us, "I will not forget you! See, I have engraved you on the palms of my hands; your walls are ever before me." Believe in his promises, and let yourself fall into his waiting arms without fear.

HIGHLIGHT

Faith isn't believing that God can—it's knowing he will.

SAVING

Why were the disciples wrong to be afraid?

because they did not have faith in God!

What is the difference between the disciples' lack of faith and Kim's lack of faith?

Kim did not have faith in humans who make mistakes. The disciples did not have faith in God who will never drop us!

Why doesn't it make sense for us to be fearful?

because God is so mighty and powerful, we are to fear him.

Rules with Reason

"Hey, Ang!" Jeffrey said. "Come to my party tonight! It's gonna be wild!"

"I can't," Angela said.

"Why not? Have you got other plans?"

"No," Angie began. "I just shouldn't go against—"

"Wait, don't tell me," Jeffrey said, holding up his hand. "It's against the rules, right?" Jeffrey said.

"They're not always easy to live with," Angie admitted. "I do want to go to your party, just like I do want to look at your illegal copy of tomorrow's chemistry test."

"So why don't you?"

"Because getting drunk at a party and cheating on a test are both things God would disapprove of."

"What does God care?" Jeffrey said, rising to leave.

"He gave us rules for a reason, Jeff," Angie said.

"What reason?" Jeffrey asked. "So you can sit around by yourself while everyone else has a good time?" He turned and walked away without waiting for an answer.

DOWNLOAD BIBLE BYTE

You must obey my laws and be careful to follow my decrees. I am the Lord your God.
Leviticus 18:4

Processing

Rules. It seems like they're everywhere, and usually they're not much fun to follow. As children we used to question why parents enforced so many rules. "They're for your own good," they'd always say. At the time this answer didn't give us any satisfaction, but looking back we can see how fooling around with matches or playing in the road could have been dangerous for us. Our parents really *were* looking out for our good!

The same is true of God's rules. Some people have a tendency to see God as a stiff-lipped killjoy who wants to destroy all our fun, but nothing could be farther from the truth. Deuteronomy 4:40 says, "Keep his decrees and commands . . . so that it may go well with you and your children after you." God created rules because he loves us and wants to keep us safe.

Rather than seeing God as a policeman in the sky, we should remember that he's our father, just as the Bible says. God's role as a father includes enforcing rules and disciplining us, but the motivation behind his discipline is love. As Proverbs 3:12 says, "The Lord disciplines those he loves, as a father the son he delights in."

HIGHLIGHT

"For your own good" is just another way of saying "because I love you."

SAVING

How do God's rules keep us from harm?

because God knows what will happen + he wants to keep us safe & out of trouble because he ♡ us!

Why are some rules so unpleasant to follow?

because it might be something we want or want to do really bad, but in the end God knows we won't need it!

How does God act as our father?

he has rules for us + loves us and wants to keep us from harm + out of trouble!

Salvation Simplified

"Through Jesus Christ we have redemption!" the pastor proclaimed. "He was the atoning sacrifice for our sins, and because of his death we have been saved!"

Scott jumped in his seat as the man beside him shouted "Amen!" A few listeners clapped as the pastor went on, and Scott studied their smiling faces. Every time the pastor mentioned "redemption" or "salvation," the congregation erupted with applause and shouts of agreement. *Salvation from what?* Scott wondered.

When the sermon ended, Scott leaned back in his seat. The notepad he'd been holding in his lap was blank except for a giant question mark he'd scribbled in the middle of the page.

"What'd you think?"

Scott looked up at the sound of Brian's voice. He shrugged his shoulders and handed the notebook to his friend. "What part of the sermon confused you?" Brian asked.

"All of it," Scott said. "I felt like the pastor was speaking a different language. Can't someone explain salvation to me in words I understand?"

DOWNLOAD BIBLE BYTE

For God so loved the world that he gave his one and only Son, that whoever believes in him shall not perish but have eternal life.
John 3:16

Processing

Are you unsure about what it means to be "saved"? Do you understand salvation but have difficulty making it clear for others? If you answered yes to either question, read on.

What do we need to be saved from? Our sins. Everyone has sinned against God (Psalm 14:3), and our sins condemn us to eternity in hell (Romans 6:23). If we don't receive God's forgiveness for our sins, we can't live with him in heaven.

How can we be saved? Jesus, God's Son, came to earth and died as a sacrifice for the sins of all who believe in him. In order to be saved, we have to believe in Jesus and ask for God's forgiveness. Acts 10:43 says, "Everyone who believes in [Jesus] receives forgiveness of sins."

What happens when we're saved? "God has given us eternal life, and this life is in his Son" (John 5:11). Jesus' death makes us right with God. Being saved means we have a personal relationship with God. Not only do we get to spend eternity with him in heaven, but he also loves, comforts, and guides us while we're on earth.

Don't be discouraged by complicated sermons and confusing questions. Remember these basics of salvation: we're all sinners in need of forgiveness; Jesus died for our sins; belief in Jesus brings us forgiveness and eternal life with God.

HIGHLIGHT

Jesus' death paid the penalty for your sins. Believe in him and you'll be saved.

SAVING

What did Scott need to be saved from?

Sin

How do we receive God's forgiveness?

accept him as our Lord + Savior

What does it mean to have a personal relationship with God?

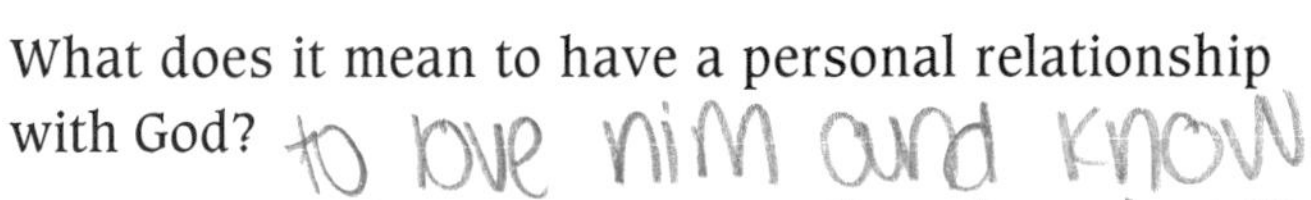

to love him and know that he loves us and to grow in his word everyday

A Helping Hand

Tracy's hands trembled so much she couldn't even read her notes as she waited backstage. She squeezed her eyes closed and focused on Principal Larson's deep voice as he tried to quiet the students.

Tracy had wanted to turn down the principal's invitation to speak at the drinking awareness assembly. She'd always been afraid of public speaking, especially when the audience consisted of eight hundred high school students. But as the president of her school's SADD (Students Against Drunk Driving) club, Tracy knew it was her responsibility to speak.

The students finally quieted down, and Principal Larson introduced Tracy. A rush of adrenaline jolted through her, but she refused to panic. "God, if you weren't going to help me, you wouldn't have put me here, right?" With that thought in mind, she breathed a prayer for courage and stepped onto the stage. As hundreds of eyes watched her approach the microphone, Tracy's hands stopped trembling.

DOWNLOAD BIBLE BYTE

The Lord said to him, "Who gave man his mouth? Who makes him deaf or mute? Who gives him sight or makes him blind? Is it not I, the Lord? Now go; I will help you speak and will teach you what to say."

Exodus 4:11–12

Processing

Moses didn't feel equipped for what God had asked him to do. He'd been commanded to tell the elders of Israel that he'd been chosen to lead the Israelites out of slavery in Egypt. Moses didn't believe he could convince the Israelites of God's plan. He expressed his fear to God, saying, "O Lord, I have never been eloquent. . . . I am slow of speech and tongue" (Exodus 4:10).

God's answer to Moses was simple: "I made you and I'll help you, so get going." God gives us tasks that might seem overwhelming but he also gives us everything we need to complete those tasks. It may have been true that Moses wasn't a good speaker, so God gave him power to perform miraculous signs. He also gave him a companion, Aaron, to speak to the people.

God doesn't tell us to do something and then let us fail. Throughout history, God has used ordinary people to do extraordinary things. He may not speak to us through burning bushes like he did with Moses (Exodus 3), but he's the same God he's always been. Don't be afraid of the responsibilities placed before you. Trust that the Maker of every talent will give you the gifts and resources you need.

HIGHLIGHT

Remember the Maker of your abilities, and turn "I can't" into "God can."

SAVING

When has the fear of failure affected your decisions?

in school, public speaking, in sports, life!

What is one "impossible" task that you've had?

I dont really know if I have really thought of any task as "impossible".

How did you handle it?

- I would pray and ask God for the strength and courage I need!

Significance beyond Understanding

Michelle spread her blanket over the dew-covered grass and rolled onto her back. Overhead, the night sky sparkled with millions of distant stars and planets. Michelle squinted, willing herself to see even deeper into the recesses of outer space.

The night was clear, the canopy of stars three-dimensional, and Michelle could see a hazy cloud-like formation stretching from one end of the sky to the other.

"The Milky Way," she noted, wondering how many other galaxies were out there.

"You created all this, God," she whispered in awe. "Can the Creator of something so great really care about someone so small?" Suddenly Michelle gasped as a shooting star streaked across the canvas of space. Its beauty brought tears to her eyes, and she smiled. "Thank you, Father," she whispered, knowing God had just answered her question.

DOWNLOAD BIBLE BYTE

"Are not five sparrows sold for two pennies? Yet not one of them is forgotten by God. Indeed, the very hairs of your head are all numbered. Don't be afraid; you are worth more than many sparrows."
Luke 12:6–7

Processing

When we consider how many people are around the globe, sometimes we feel like a number. It's easy to question our significance when most of the earth's population will never know we exist. And what about God? He has millions of followers. Does he really see every one of us? Is he aware of every thought and feeling we experience?

Yes! God sees us inside and out, twenty-four hours a day. Isaiah 49:15-16 says, "Can a mother forget the baby at her breast? . . . Though she may forget, I will not forget you! See, I have engraved you on the palms of my hands; your walls are ever before me." God doesn't call us his children only because he created us. He literally plays the role of a loving father. He knows and loves each child individually, and though he sees the whole world, he never takes his eyes off his individual children.

It's impossible for us to comprehend how God can know millions of us intimately, but he's God. He can do anything! Though it seems impossible, we're significant to the Creator of the universe. We're loved so deeply that he's numbered the hairs on our heads and given us the beauty of night skies, including shooting stars!

SAVING

When have you ever felt insignificant?

I believe that I have always known that God loves + knows each of us.

Why does being a Christian make us significant?

God calls us his "children"

How does knowledge of God's constant attention affect our behavior?

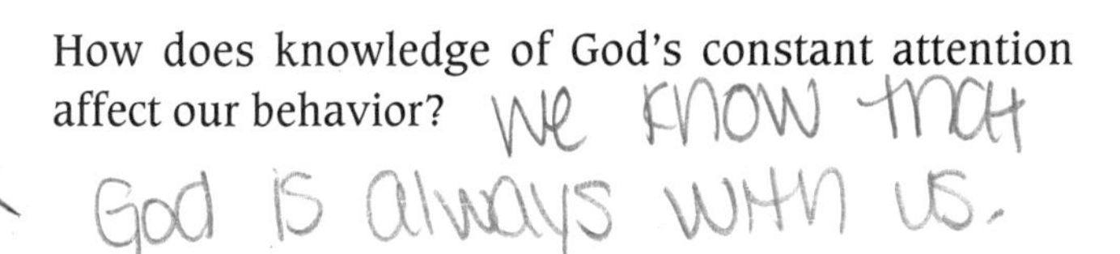

Anchored in Hope

"Good morning," Doug said cheerfully as his sister entered the kitchen. Grunting in response, Brandy stumbled to the table and collapsed into a chair. "Uh-oh," Doug said. "What is it this time?"

"What do you think?" Brandy snapped, annoyed at her brother's careless attitude. Doug sighed. He knew he should be more sensitive, but Brandy's mood swings were hard to handle. She was wildly happy one minute and unbearably depressed the next. And Doug knew the reason for her ups and downs: Bill Hughes.

"Did Bill upset you again?" he asked, trying to sound sympathetic. Brandy nodded her head slowly, and Doug could see she was battling tears.

"I get so hopeful that he's changed, but he keeps disappointing me," she said. She went on to tell Doug about how Bill had hurt her. "I need to stop placing my hope in him," she finally admitted. "Every time he pulls me up, I know he's going to pull me back down any moment."

DOWNLOAD BIBLE BYTE

We have this hope as an anchor for the soul, firm and secure.
Hebrews 6:19

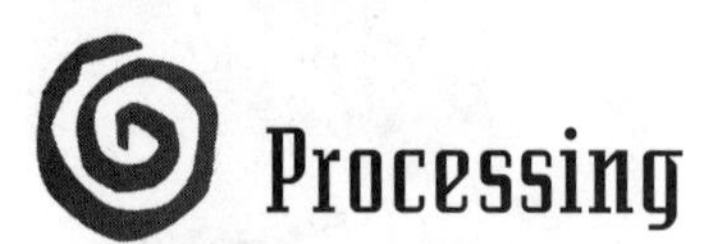

Processing

The purpose of an anchor is to hold a boat in one place. Without an anchor, the boat is at the mercy of the waves and current. It goes wherever the unpredictable sea takes it. But an anchor grounds the boat and protects it from crashing against the rocks or drifting into unsafe waters.

In a world of ups and downs, we're constantly searching for an anchor to cling to. We put our hope in many things, including money, health, and relationships, but all these things eventually fail us. They're like the waves, lifting us up one minute, and crashing us against the rocks the next. Like Brandy, sometimes our happiness is fleeting because the things we hope in are fleeting.

There is only one hope that can be trusted as a firm and secure anchor: God. He holds us steady in his love, and he'll never disappoint us. We're safe from destruction because he is more powerful than the most turbulent sea. Nothing can uproot him or pull us away from him. "Find rest, O my soul, in God alone; my hope comes from him. He alone is my rock and my salvation; he is my fortress, I will not be shaken" (Psalm 62:5–6).

HIGHLIGHT

Whether the waters of life are calm or rough, hope in God is an anchor that cannot be uprooted.

SAVING

What "waves" have failed you in the past?

Skool, grades, friends

Why aren't those things like an anchor?

they are not always giving me what I need

Why is God the only true source of hope?

he is a mighty + loving God!

The Daily Surrender

When his phone rang at 7 P.M., Adam was walking toward the living room holding a TV dinner in one hand and a rented video in the other. He let the answering machine pick up and listened as Corey's voice came on the speaker.

"Natalie Spencer just called me," Corey said. "Her lawn mower is messed up and I told her you and I could probably fix it. Give me a call if you can help out." The machine beeped as Corey hung up, and Adam collapsed into an easy chair. *Why tonight?* He tossed the video aside, took a few bites of his lukewarm dinner, and grabbed the phone.

"Corey," he said when his friend answered. "It's Adam."

"Hey," Corey said. "How've you been?"

"Busy," he replied. "This is my first night to relax in two weeks."

"So you probably don't feel like making a trip to Natalie's?"

"Yeah, well, that's what I called about," Adam said, and sighed. "There will be other nights. What time should I pick you up?"

DOWNLOAD BIBLE BYTE

Then he said to them all: "If anyone would come after me, he must deny himself and take up his cross daily and follow me."
Luke 9:23

Processing

What is self-denial? Some people think denying self is about giving up pleasure or refusing to meet personal needs. But when Jesus told his disciples to deny themselves, he didn't mean they should neglect their own desires and needs. He was asking them for a willingness to put him first.

Selfishness comes naturally to us. The first sin was an act of selfishness—Eve put *her* desire ahead of *God's* command, and ever since then humans have been doing the same thing. Self-denial is about saying no to self and yes to God. It's hard, and it's not a decision we can make once and for all. Self-denial is a daily surrender to the desires of God.

How do we know when we're putting God first? Comparing our lives to the Bible's standards is the best way to determine whether we're serving ourselves or God. He's commanded us to love our neighbors, give to the needy, and resist temptations to sin. When Adam denied his desire for a night to himself in order to help Natalie, he put God before himself. That's the kind of self-denial Jesus spoke of in Luke 9:23.

> **HIGHLIGHT**
>
> "We are all serving a life sentence in the dungeon of self."
> —Cyril Connolly, English literary critic

SAVING

When is self-denial pleasing to God?

when we give up our own wants for what God wants.

How have you denied yourself recently?

?

Why can't we choose to deny ourselves once and for all?

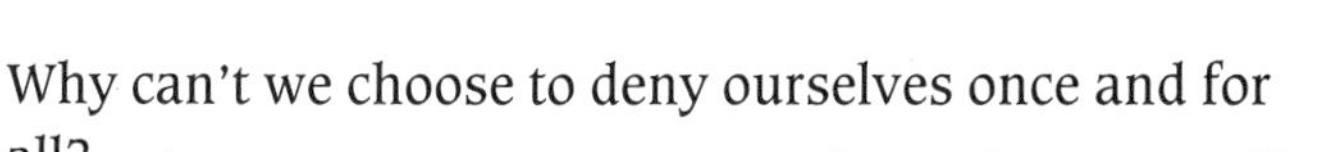

Fearing Our God

Tiffany frowned at her car stereo and switched the power off. She didn't understand the on-air sermon, and listening to it was upsetting her. "Fear the Lord," the preacher kept saying, but Tiffany didn't want to fear God. *He's the only thing I'm not afraid of,* she thought, thinking of her father.

Tiffany's father had physically abused her and her mother since she could remember. Every time Tiffany walked into her house she was overcome by fear of what the man would do. If the mood hit him, he could be provoked to violence without warning. The thought of fearing God as she feared her hot-tempered father was disturbing to Tiffany. *God is supposed to love me, so why should I fear him?* She wondered. She turned the stereo back on, hoping the preacher would take back his words so she could once again feel safe in her relationship with God.

DOWNLOAD BIBLE BYTE

But be sure to fear the Lord and serve him faithfully with all your heart; consider what great things he has done for you.

1 Samuel 12:24

Processing

When we think of fear, we usually imagine a sense of dread, as though something harmful might happen to us. Fear strips us of security and makes us want to run and hide from the source of our fright. Tiffany had experienced this kind of fear because of her abusive father. When she was told to fear God, who is supposed to be loving, Tiffany was confused.

Tiffany isn't alone. Many of us have trouble with the concept of fearing God. Some think we should fear God because of the threat of hell, but Christ already rescued us from our sin, so there's no reason to be afraid of hell.

What Tiffany didn't realize is that fear of God isn't like other fears. Rather than causing us to hide in terror, it makes us bow before him in respect and draw closer to him in awe. We fear God as we consider his power and majesty, and we show our fear by obeying his commands (Deuteronomy 6:2). Tiffany was terrified of her father because of what he had done *to* her. We fear God because of what he does *for* us. It is God's greatness, not his wrath, that inspires our fear and obedience.

HIGHLIGHT

Fear of God is the only fear that makes us safe and secure for eternity.

SAVING

What is the difference between Tiffany's fear of her father and fear of God? her father is abusive and dangerous but God loves us + is mighty + powerfull

What causes you to fear God?

i really have never thought about this ? ?

How do we show our fear of God?

we praise him + worship him + respect + draw closer to him.

Dressed for Battle

"Dear Mom," Shelby wrote. "By the time you read this, I'll be gone." She paused and shifted in the seat, lifting her paralyzed legs onto a stool to ease the pain in her back.

"You say suicide is wrong," she continued, "but it would also be wrong for me to keep living." Shelby reached for a tissue and dabbed at the tears that blurred her vision.

"Mom, I've been a burden since I was born. My existence doesn't do anything but make everyone's life more difficult."

She set down the pen and reached for her prescription pain pills. There were twenty-two left in the bottle, and she poured them all out on the table. Her head pounded as opposing feelings battled within her. "Take them," one voice said, while the other whispered, "Don't give up."

DOWNLOAD BIBLE BYTE

Put on the full armor of God, so that you can take your stand against the devil's schemes. For our struggle is not against flesh and blood, but against the . . . spiritual forces of evil in the heavenly realms.

Ephesians 6:11–12

Processing

We're all involved in a war. It's the battle of good versus evil, and Christians are soldiers in God's army against Satan and the "spiritual forces of evil." We can't see Satan working, but like Shelby we can feel his attacks through the sorrow, heartache, and temptation in our lives.

Ephesians 6:14–18 tells us God offers his soldiers the belt of truth, the breastplate of righteousness, the shield of faith, the helmet of salvation, the sword of the Spirit, and prayer. This equipment is described as "full armor," meaning that it covers us from head to toe. If we put on the full armor of God, Satan can't break through to harm us.

We feel Satan's attacks because we don't always wear our armor or use it correctly. Just like real soldiers, we have to learn to defend ourselves. The lessons that teach us to fight properly can be painful, but we have to go through them to learn how to protect ourselves. Each attack teaches us how to hold up the shield of faith and ward off blows with the sword of the Spirit. And as we learn the lessons of war, we can be confident in the promise of Romans 16:19–20: "Be wise about what is good, and innocent about what is evil. The God of peace will soon crush Satan under your feet."

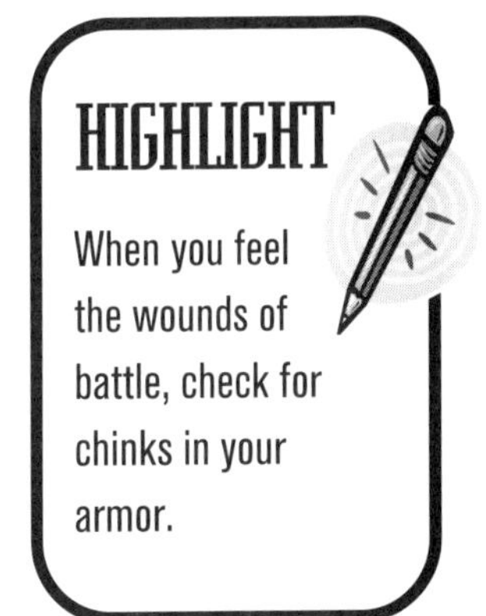

SAVING

When have you felt like you were in a battle?

in school, in my spiritual life + many other times

What is the armor of God? (Read Ephesians 6:14–18.)

What is the purpose of our struggles against evil forces? Only to make us stronger!

Wrongful Worship

Joy sank onto the couch with the latest issue of *Elegance.* The magazine had been a week late arriving. Joy had almost bought it at the supermarket, but one of her friends showed up with a copy at school. That had satisfied Joy until her issue arrived.

Flipping to the middle of the magazine, Joy studied the prom preview section. Longing filled her as she studied the breathtaking models. *I'd give anything to look like that*, she thought. Turning the page, Joy spotted the most beautiful evening gown she'd ever seen. Running her fingers reverently over the page, she imagined herself wrapped in the expensive velvet. She'd never own such a fancy dress, but Joy couldn't help imagining a different life for herself.

After a few minutes, Joy threw the magazine aside with a frustrated sigh. She wanted more than anything to be beautiful like those models or rich enough to own those clothes. *I'd die to be like them*, she thought.

DOWNLOAD BIBLE BYTE

They exchanged the truth of God for a lie, and worshiped and served created things rather than the Creator—who is forever praised. Amen.
Romans 1:25

Processing

Paul, the writer of Romans, lived in a society of idolatry. Citizens and slaves of the Roman Empire visited temples, made sacrifices, and carried images of false gods. Their idols symbolized love, sexual pleasure, strength, and fertility, among other things.

Today's society doesn't practice the obvious idolatry of the Roman Empire, but we still have idols. Our society worships personal gratification. Rather than visiting temples or making animal sacrifices, we devote ourselves to the pursuit of wealth, beauty, and pleasure. We're told to "do what feels good," and fulfill our own desires, no matter what the cost. WRONG!

God is no more pleased by modern idolatry than the idolatry of the Romans. He doesn't want to share our hearts with false gods. God commands, "You shall have no other gods before me. . . . You shall not bow down to them or worship them; for I, the Lord your God, am a jealous God" (Exodus 20:3, 5).

It's important for us to recognize the idolatry of our time. Even Christians aren't immune to the subtle worship of false gods. We also desire wealth, beauty, and pleasure. In our pursuit of personal fulfillment, let's remember God alone can meet our needs and offer us the satisfaction we so desperately seek.

HIGHLIGHT

Our God is a jealous God. He wants every inch of our hearts to be devoted only to him.

SAVING

What are some idols in your life?

friends, boys, phone, aol, clothes,

Why are idols ultimately a sham?

because they can never turn out like God!

Why is God displeased when we seek wealth and beauty?

because our eyes are supposed to be focused on him!

A New Perspective

"God, what do you want me to do?"

Suzanne was tired of asking for God's guidance. She had to make a decision about college, but after weeks of praying she still didn't have an answer.

Suzanne picked up her phone and considered calling Alexa. *If only I knew God as well as I know my best friend*, she thought. Suzanne and Alexa could finish one another's sentences. Their deep friendship had developed over years of companionship. Suzanne knew Alexa well enough to read her mind.

But Suzanne was seeking God's will, not Alexa's. Suzanne sighed and put the phone down. *Why can't I read God's mind the way I can read Alexa's?*

DOWNLOAD BIBLE BYTE

Do not conform any longer to the pattern of this world, but be transformed by the renewing of your mind. Then you will be able to test and approve what God's will is—his good, pleasing and perfect will.
Romans 12:2

Processing

"What is God's will for my life?" All Christians ask themselves this question. As we face decisions about relationships, education, and career paths, we're constantly looking for road signs to direct us along the way. Unfortunately, following God's route isn't as easy as driving down the interstate. Sometimes God, in his wisdom, chooses to keep his will hidden. But even when he puts "road signs" right in front of us, we often drive by without noticing.

We're blinded to God's will because our minds have been corrupted by sin. We live in a world that's "under the control of the evil one" (1 John 5:19), and as sinful people we've conformed to the world's patterns. If we want to know God's will, we have to see our lives with a new perspective. Being "transformed by the renewing of your mind" means we learn to view our lives through God's eyes.

How do you renew your mind? Get to know God. Pray, read the Bible, and learn about God's love, purity, justice, and righteousness. Suzanne spent countless hours with Alexa until she could almost read her friend's mind. If we hope to know God's will, we have to spend time learning who he is. As we discover God's character and embrace our relationship with him, we'll be transformed. The road signs will be easier to see when we search for them with renewed minds.

SAVING

Who do you know better: God or your best friend?

In different ways, I know God better, and in different ways I know my best friend better. I should in all ways know God better.

How have you conformed to the world's patterns?

Do not become part of the world!!

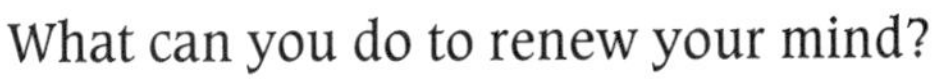

What can you do to renew your mind?

talk to God, read his word - spend time with God!!

Bench-Pressing for God

Jack saw the tackle coming and knew before he hit the ground that he'd be out for the season. The pain in his knee was too intense to be a minor injury, and the doctor soon confirmed that he'd need surgery.

Lying in his bed the next morning, Jack sighed in frustration. His alarm had gone off early even though it was a Saturday. He hadn't turned it off the night before, forgetting he wouldn't go jogging in the morning like he usually did.

Life looks different lying down, Jack thought. After months of training, he'd finally become a starting running back for varsity. He'd made football his life to be ready by preseason practice, and now all the running and weightlifting seemed worthless. *What good do speed and strength do me now?* He wondered. It no longer mattered that his teammates considered him one of the strongest players. Jack felt like the weakest person alive as he lay helplessly in bed, watching the sunrise.

DOWNLOAD BIBLE BYTE

For physical training is of some value, but godliness has value for all things, holding promise for both the present life and the life to come.
1 Timothy 4:8

Processing

The Greeks of Timothy's time loved to train their bodies. They were especially interested in gymnastic exercises, and the most talented athletes were honored among the people. But Timothy warned the Greeks that their definition of strength wouldn't stand up to the test of time.

We live in a physical world where strength is linked with muscular endurance, athletic ability, and health. But Psalm 73:26 reminds us that true power has nothing to do with these things: "My flesh and my heart may fail, but God is the strength of my heart and my portion forever." We take vitamins, go jogging, and lift weights to feel strong and healthy, yet our physical strength will eventually fail us.

Physical strength is beneficial and we should try to stay healthy, but we should resist the temptation to place physical condition above spiritual condition. Jack neglected everything, including his relationship with God, to train for football season. Physical strength became the most important thing in his life, and when it was taken from him he was left with nothing. Instead of following Jack's example, focus your attention on building your spiritual "muscles." Spend time getting to know God. The strength he offers will last for eternity.

HIGHLIGHT

Both physical muscles and spiritual muscles have to be "worked out" in order to grow, but only spiritual muscles last forever.

SAVING

What's the danger in trusting solely in your physical strength? it will eventually let you down- God won't!

Why did Jack feel weak?

because he had been on the bench for a while

What's the difference between physical and spiritual strength? physical strength is not honoring God & spiritual strength is honoring God.

Eternal Treasure

Andrea's room looked like a tornado had blown through it. Her clothes were everywhere, spilling from dresser drawers, hanging off the closet doors, strewn across the bed and floor. But Andrea was more concerned with her jewelry box, which lay upside down on the bedspread. *Please be there,* she begged no one in particular, frantically searching through bead necklaces and plastic bracelets. *No! They have to be here!* But they weren't. The pair of diamond earrings, Andrea's most prized possession, was gone forever.

"Andrea, did they take anything in here?" Andrea's mother asked from the doorway.

"My earrings," she replied, her voice shaking. "The pair grandma left me. They're gone, Mom!" Sinking onto her clothing-covered bed, Andrea covered her face and began to cry.

DOWNLOAD BIBLE BYTE

"But store up for yourselves treasures in heaven, where moth and rust do not destroy, and where thieves do not break in and steal. For where your treasure is, there your heart will be also."
Matthew 6:20–21

Processing

Moths eat through designer clothing, rust destroys luxury cars, and with the right plan and resources burglars can sneak past sophisticated security systems to steal our most valuable possessions. Heavenly treasures, on the other hand, cannot be eaten, destroyed, or stolen.

To treasure something is to give it an important place in our hearts. Andrea treasured the earrings because they were a reminder of her grandmother, who was also a treasure. It's understandable that Andrea would cry over losing the earrings, which had sentimental value. But her sadness should remind us to hold loosely to temporary treasures. They can be taken from us at any time, unlike heavenly treasures, which last forever.

"Treasures in heaven" are things of eternal significance, such as suffering for Christ (Matthew 5:12), prayer (Matthew 6:6), charity (Luke 18:22), hospitality (Matthew 10:42), and generosity (1 Timothy 6:18–19). Jesus himself is an eternal treasure that can give us eternal life. How do we treasure Christ? "If you love me, you will obey what I command," he said in John 14:15. Jesus wants us to treasure him, follow him, and store up treasures in heaven where we will one day see him face to face.

HIGHLIGHT

Heavenly treasures are costless acts with priceless value.

SAVING

How do we know when something is a treasure to us? when it means a lot to us and we know that if it were to get lost, we would be heartbroken.

What are your temporary treasures?

?

Why are treasures in heaven more important than earthly treasures? because they can not be destroyed + ~~you don't~~ where the treasure is, there your heart will be also.

Fearless Love

Shelly took a deep breath before exiting her car. The speeding ticket crumpled in her hand was moist from her clammy skin. *Relax, Shel,* she told herself. *It's not like he's going to throw you out on the street.*

Shelly knew her father would be furious when he found out she'd gotten another speeding ticket. It was only the second one, but after last time her father had warned her to slow down.

Shelly finally left the car and walked to her front door. She saw her father through the window sitting in his favorite chair, reading the newspaper. The familiar sight comforted Shelly as she entered the house. *He's the same dad he's always been*, she told herself, thinking about how many times her father had proven his love for her over the last sixteen years. No, he wouldn't be happy about the ticket, but Shelly reminded herself that nothing could make him stop loving her.

DOWNLOAD BIBLE BYTE

There is no fear in love. But perfect love drives out fear, because fear has to do with punishment. The one who fears is not made perfect in love.
1 John 4:18

Processing

The love we feel from parents or close friends usually goes hand in hand with a feeling of safety. We're secure in that love because it's supposed to be unconditional, or perfect. Like Shelly, we trust that no matter what happens, that person will always love us.

Of course, no human love is perfect because the human race is *im*perfect. Only God offers us truly unconditional love, and this study's Bible Byte is about his love. Romans 8:38–39 says that, "neither death nor life, neither angels nor demons, neither the present nor the future, nor any powers, neither height nor depth, nor anything else in all creation, will be able to separate us from the love of God that is in Christ Jesus our Lord." If nothing can take God's love for us away, what do we have to fear?

Fear and perfect love can't occupy the same space at the same time. The love of God our Father is perfect love, so our hearts can't be held captive by fear as long as we trust in his love. He has saved us through the death and resurrection of Christ. We have no need to fear the punishment of hell because Jesus has paid the price for our sins. And if we don't need to fear the horrors of hell, why should we fear anything? God's perfect love will remain with us through eternity, driving away fear as we walk securely with him.

SAVING

What are you most afraid of?

seperation of friends + family
-heaven + hell

Who in your life do you believe loves you unconditionally? my mom + dad

Why does perfect love drive out fear?

because we know that even if we mess up, they will still love us.

Saved . . . Once and for All

Samantha dug her fingernails into the carpet as she knelt beside her bed. "Forgive me, Lord," she pleaded. "I failed you again today."

With trembling lips she began confessing her sins. "I was rude to Mom this morning. I gossiped about Suzanne." The list seemed endless, and nausea washed over Samantha as she prayed. "I lied to my coach. I yelled at . . ." She slapped a hand over her mouth as the nausea worsened, sending chills through her arms and legs. Gradually the sensation passed, and Samantha felt tears pushing from behind her eyes.

"Please don't leave me, God," she cried suddenly. "I know I keep sinning, but I'm trying to get better. Don't leave me!" Sweat beaded and streamed down her forehead, mingling with the tears on her flushed cheeks.

She hunched over and pressed her shaking hands over her eyes. "I'm sorry, Lord! Please don't stop loving me."

DOWNLOAD BIBLE BYTE

"I give them eternal life, and they shall never perish; no one can snatch them out of my hand. My Father, who has given them to me, is greater than all; no one can snatch them out of my Father's hand."
John 10:28

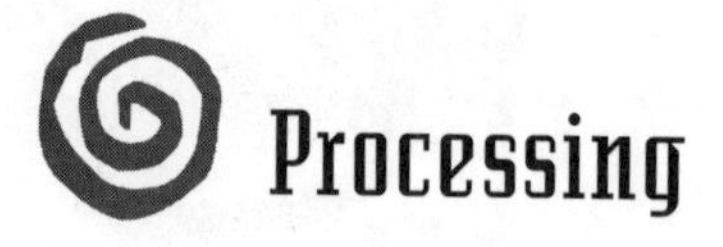

Processing

Jesus died to pay the penalty for our sins. When we believe in him and ask for God's forgiveness, we're saved. Our salvation from sin means we have the promise of eternal life. Samantha thought she understood salvation, but she still wondered if she could be separated from God once she was saved.

According to Jesus, no one can snatch a believer away from God. Once he's opened his hands to us, we remain in his grasp forever. Psalm 103:17 says, "From everlasting to everlasting, the Lord's love is with those who fear him." Samantha worried that her continued sin would separate her from God, but when God forgives us, he forgives *everything*. Past, present, and future sins are wiped away by the blood of Christ.

God's complete forgiveness doesn't give us an excuse to sin when we feel like it. True salvation requires a repentant heart, meaning we have to be sorry for our sins. As true followers of God, we'll try to avoid sin, but when we make mistakes, God won't hold them against us. In the words of Romans 8:38–39, "Neither the present nor the future . . . will be able to separate us from the love of God that is in Christ Jesus our Lord."

HIGHLIGHT

God can see your life from beginning to end. When he forgives your sins, he forgives the past, present, and future.

SAVING

What didn't Samantha understand about God's love?

Gods love is everlasting + he will never stop loving us.

Why were her worries unfounded?

Why shouldn't Christians take God's complete forgiveness for granted? because if we did

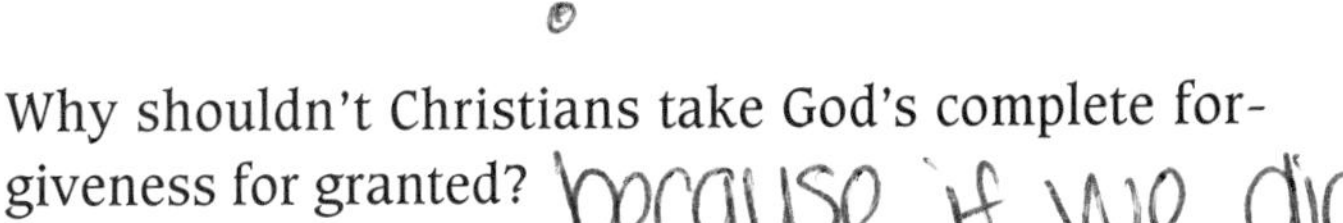

+ forgiveness.

Vital Connection

"You used to enjoy working here, Caroline," Macy said. "What's changed?" Caroline shrugged and yanked the sheets off another bed.

"It's a nursing home. What is there to enjoy?" Even though her tone was negative, Caroline knew her coworker was right. There'd been a time when the job was fulfilling, but lately it was just a job keeping her from the things she really enjoyed.

Pulling out some fresh sheets, Caroline sighed. The nursing home wasn't her only problem. She wasn't happy with anything anymore, and each day she became more unsatisfied.

As she made the bed, Caroline noticed a plaque on the wall. A Bible verse was engraved on it, reminding Caroline that she hadn't opened her Bible in months. *I haven't done a lot of things in months*, she thought, *including pray*.

DOWNLOAD BIBLE BYTE

"I am the vine; you are the branches. If a man remains in me and I in him, he will bear much fruit; apart from me you can do nothing."
John 15:5

Processing

Jesus uses this illustration to describe our dependency on him. Like the vine or stem of a plant, Jesus is our source of nourishment. He's the lifeline carrying essential nutrients needed by the plant. As "branches," we're directly connected to Jesus, and through him we receive food, so we can produce fruit.

Galatians 5:22 tells about the fruit that should grow on our branches: "The fruit of the spirit is love, joy, peace, patience, kindness, goodness, faithfulness, gentleness and self-control." If we remain in Christ, our lives will be filled with the fruit of the spirit, showing others that we're connected to Jesus (John 15:8).

Apart from the vine, branches don't have enough food to bear fruit or even survive. Caroline neglected her relationship with Christ, and she saw the effects in her life. The peace and joy she'd felt, as well as the kindness she'd shown to others, was replaced by discontentment and selfishness.

Without our vital connection to Jesus, our souls would wither and harden like dead branches. We'd fail to produce the fruit of the spirit, and there wouldn't be any evidence of life flowing through us. We can avoid ending up in Caroline's shoes by nurturing our relationship with Christ. He'll give us everything we need to grow strong and produce the fruit of his spirit.

HIGHLIGHT

Jesus is the source of spiritual life. Guard your connection to him above all else.

SAVING

Have you ever felt discouraged the way Caroline did?

yes!

What are the long-term effects of disconnection from Christ? living a non-christian life & going to hell

How can you remain connected to the vine?

read his word, talk with God, be an example for others - born again!

Angelic Encounter

Trudy's breath came in gasps as she hurried down the alleyway. Shadows reached out to her from all sides, and her skin crawled at every sound. *How did I let myself get lost?* Turning a corner, Trudy's heart sank as she found it was another dead end. *Where am I?* She closed her eyes. *God, help me!*

"Hello, Trudy." Trudy's eyes shot open at the stranger's voice. She started to back away from him.

"Don't be afraid," the man said. "I'm here to help."

Trudy listened in amazement as the man told her how to escape the alley. He spoke slowly, and his soft voice soothed her. "Go now," he told her. "You'll be safe." Trudy started to leave, but then turned back toward him.

"Thank . . ." she began, but the man was already gone. Trudy spun around, searching for a retreating figure, but she was alone. *How'd he know my name? Who on earth? . . .* Then she remembered her prayer. *An angel?*

DOWNLOAD BIBLE BYTE

For he will command his angels concerning you to guard you in all your ways; they will lift you up in their hands, so that you will not strike your foot against a stone.
Psalm 91:11–12

Processing

It seems like angels are everywhere these days. They decorate notecards and wrapping paper, hang from strings on rearview mirrors, and sit on top of Christmas trees during the holidays. But what about *real* angels? Was Trudy crazy to think the helpful stranger was an angel sent from God?

The Bible tells us about angels serving God in many ways. They delivered messages (Genesis 16), helped God's followers (1 Kings 19), and praised God (Luke 2:13). But are angels still at work around us? The Bible never tells us God stopped using his angels to communicate with us and help us, but most people still think of them as imaginary, rosy-cheeked babies with wings. However, angels in the Bible often appeared as common men (Genesis 18). Hebrews 13:2 says, "Do not forget to entertain strangers, for by so doing some people have entertained angels without knowing it."

Maybe Trudy wasn't crazy after all. What do you think? Maybe Trudy met an angel, maybe not. The important thing to remember is this: nothing is impossible for God, and the mysterious stranger, angel or no angel, was an answer to Trudy's prayer.

HIGHLIGHT

Angels aren't just plastic figurines on the tops of Christmas trees. Keep your eyes open for the real thing!

SAVING

Have you ever had an experience like Trudy's?

yes!

How would you respond if a friend told you they'd encountered an angel? i would ask them about what they saw... I think it would be awesome to encounter an angel.

Why do you think people dismiss the existence of real angels today? because they think they are just like ghosts + witches... they don't exist - but they do!

Forgotten Blessings

Samuel tugged at his collar as he walked through the door of the sanctuary. He felt uncomfortable dressed in his Sunday best after having gone weeks without attending church. If not for his nagging depression, he probably wouldn't be here now.

Samuel had suffered for several years with chronic depression. Sometimes he could go for months on end and feel nothing but contentment. But then he'd wake up one morning without any desire to go on living. At those times he turned to God for help.

I only talk to God when I need something, Samuel realized with a pang of guilt. Whenever his prayers were answered, Samuel was always too caught up in feeling good again to remember who was responsible for his recovery.

Processing

No matter what kind of trouble the Israelites faced, God always helped them out of it. When they were slaves in Egypt, God sent Moses to lead them to freedom. When the Israelites were hungry in the desert, God rescued them by sending quail and manna to fill their stomachs. Yet when bad times turned to good, the Israelites always forgot their dependence on God and failed to show gratitude for his blessings.

You and I have never been slaves to Pharaoh or found ourselves stranded in the desert, but sometimes

DOWNLOAD BIBLE BYTE

But I am the Lord your God, who brought you out of Egypt. . . . I cared for you in the desert, in the land of burning heat. When I fed them, they were satisfied; when they were satisfied, they became proud; then they forgot me.
Hosea 13:4–6

we act like the Israelites. In our weakness, we quickly seek his strength. But when he answers our pleas for help, it's never long before our dependency on him is forgotten.

We should be living in continual gratitude toward God. Consider what he's done for us! As if giving us eternal life through Christ isn't enough, God has also invited us to a personal relationship with him. We can speak directly to the Creator of the universe, and he gives us comfort, peace, and joy because he *loves* us. "Praise the Lord, O my soul, and forget not all his benefits—who forgives all your sins and heals all your diseases, . . . who satisfies your desires with good things" (Psalm 103:2–3, 5).

SAVING

When do you pray?

Every night

Do you relate to the Israelites?

in certain ways

What are some things God has already given you?

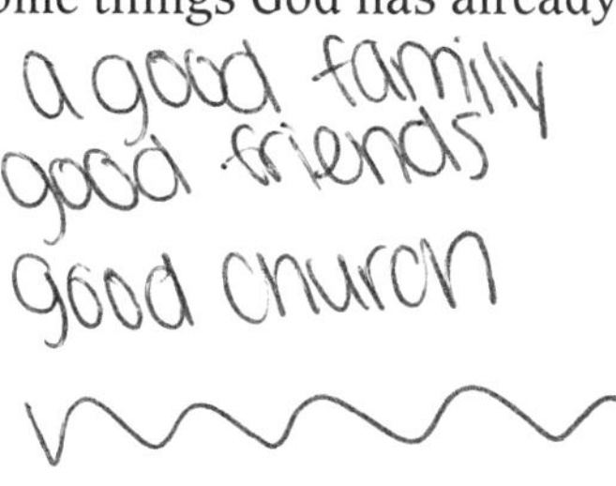

Swapping Masters

"Come to the shore with me Sunday," Larry said, taking a seat on Gabe's bed.

"I can't," Gabe said from the computer. "I've got church." Larry shook his head as he watched his friend type.

A Bible sat on Gabe's bed, and Larry picked it up. He opened to a bookmarked page and scanned the highlighted verses. When he realized what he was looking at, Larry chuckled. *Figures,* he thought. *The Ten Commandments.*

"What's so funny?" Gabe asked.

"Why do you follow this?" Larry asked, pointing at the Bible. "What do you get from God that's worth putting up with all his rules?"

Gabe considered Larry's question. "Freedom," he finally said.

"Freedom?" Larry laughed, then shook his head. "Seems to me you're more of a slave than a free man."

Gabe's slow smile took him by surprise. "Yeah, maybe," Gabe said quietly. "But it's my slavery to God that sets me free."

DOWNLOAD BIBLE BYTE

"So if the Son sets you free, you will be free indeed."
John 8:36

Processing

Sometimes the Christian life feels more like a life of slavery than freedom. When we give our lives to God, we promise to follow him. While other people go around doing whatever they want, we put our desires aside and obey God's commands. In other words, we become his servants. What kind of freedom is that?

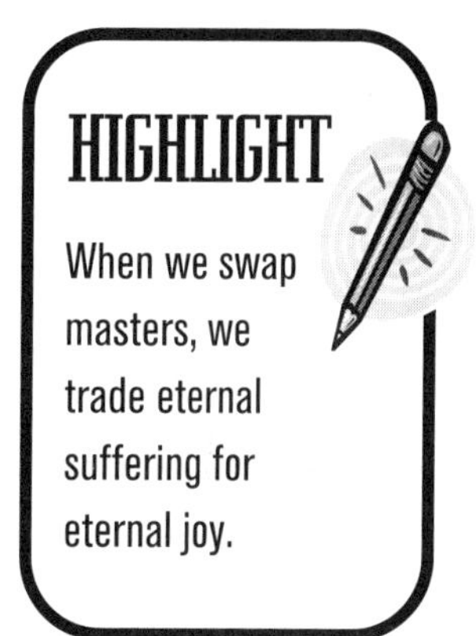

Whether we like it or not, we're all slaves to something. If we're not slaves to God, we're slaves to sin. Sin separates us from God and all the blessings that come from a personal relationship with him. The chains of sin bind us from growing into the people God wants us to be, and after death they condemn us to eternal separation from him. But when we accept Jesus as our Savior, we're freed from that fate. Romans 6:22 says, "Now that you have been set free from sin and have become slaves to God, the benefit you reap leads to holiness, and the result is eternal life."

Yes, being a Christian means we have to follow lots of rules and overlook our sinful impulses. But slavery to righteousness allows us to experience God's presence and love throughout our lives, both now and in eternity.

SAVING

The people around you are slaves to what?

their own actions + beliefs

How was Gabe's slavery different than Larry's?

Gabe's slavery. will set her free + Larry's will not.

How does slavery to God lead to freedom?

When we obey Gods word...

Wholehearted Workers

Jane crossed off the third item on the list her mother had written. There were over twenty chores on it, and Jane couldn't understand why they had to be completed today. It was Saturday, her only day to sleep in and relax. And besides, her parents were leaving on vacation. Why should they care if the house was spotless?

Turning on the vacuum, Jane ran it over the dirtiest parts of the carpet, knowing her mother wouldn't check the corners. Crossing off another task, she grabbed the window cleaner and attacked the bathroom mirror. The list said, "wash mirrors," but Jane knew no one would be using the upstairs bathroom, so she put the cleaner away and moved on. At this pace, she'd be done long before lunchtime.

Processing

Some people want high grades, so they work hard in class. Some people want higher wages, so they perform well at work. Other people like the feeling of personal satisfaction that comes from a job well done, so they put extra effort into the tasks before them. But there are always things we don't like to do, so we don't put much effort into doing them. We blow off boring homework assignments that don't really affect our grades. Or like Jane we're careless with the household chores, figuring no one will notice. If something is unpleasant and not very significant, why waste energy doing it well?

DOWNLOAD BIBLE BYTE

Whatever you do, work at it with all your heart, as working for the Lord, not for men, since you know that you will receive an inheritance from the Lord as a reward. It is the Lord Christ you are serving.
Colossians 3:23–24

The words from this study's Bible Byte were directed toward slaves. They didn't have a choice about obeying their masters, but they had a choice about how well they would do their jobs. We have the same choice when completing assignments from teachers, parents, and employers.

Sometimes it's hard to be enthusiastic about work when you think you're only serving a human authority. But this passage reminds us that our real master is God, and he expects a strong work ethic. God wants us to be wholehearted about everything. He tells us to love, serve, and obey him with all our heart (Deuteronomy 11:13; 30:2). Is it any surprise that he wants us to take the same wholehearted attitude into every area of our lives?

HIGHLIGHT

"Good is not good, where better is expected."
—Thomas Fuller, English clergyman and author

SAVING

What are some tasks you work at halfheartedly?

schoolwork, chores, friends, spending time w/ God - (quiet time)

What would God like you to do differently?

put all my effort into completing those things

What are we saying to God when we don't do our best? that its not important and that we dont care

Meaningless Wealth

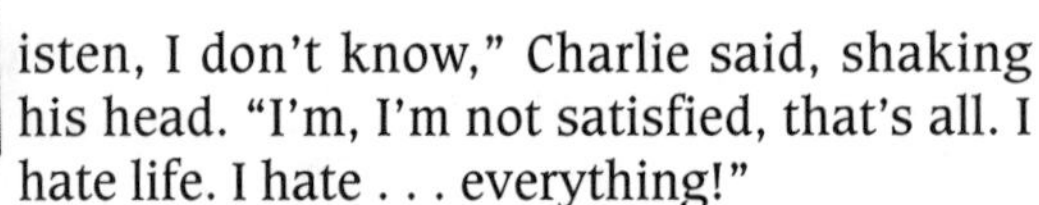

“Listen, I don’t know,” Charlie said, shaking his head. “I’m, I’m not satisfied, that’s all. I hate life. I hate . . . everything!”

“I know you’re not satisfied, Charlie, but *why* aren’t you satisfied?” The psychologist’s question made Charlie shift in the leather chair. For once he couldn’t come up with a clever answer. Charlie stared at the Rolex his dad had bought him. He still had thirty minutes with this annoying therapist.

“If you’re supposed to be so brilliant, why don’t you come up with the answer?” he finally responded.

“Okay,” the psychologist said slowly, removing her reading glasses. “I’ll give it a shot. Your father’s the richest man in the city and he’s bought you everything you could possibly want. But you want more, right?” Charlie remained silent and slouched down in his chair. “You’re not satisfied because your happiness depends on wealth,” the therapist continued. She leaned toward her scowling client. “But money doesn’t buy happiness, does it Charles?”

DOWNLOAD BIBLE BYTE

I denied myself nothing my eyes desired; I refused my heart no pleasure. . . . Yet when I surveyed all that my hands had done and what I had toiled to achieve, everything was meaningless.
Ecclesiastes 2:10–11

Processing

Solomon, the writer of Ecclesiastes, had enough wealth and power to get anything he wanted. He was the king of Israel and the richest man in the world during his reign. If happiness could be bought with money, Solomon would have been one happy guy. He had land, wives, slaves, animals, gold, and every other luxury of the rich and famous. But after acquiring everything his money could buy, Solomon concluded his possessions were meaningless. Why? Because his possessions couldn't go with him into eternity.

Solomon writes in Ecclesiastes 5:15, "Naked a man comes from his mother's womb, and as he comes, so he departs." He knew he'd have to leave every earthly possession behind when it came time to pass from this life into the next.

After seeking pleasure in the world's riches, Solomon and Charlie were both left unsatisfied. We don't know how Charlie's story ends, but we do know that Solomon eventually realized eternal wealth and fulfillment come only from God. Solomon's father, David, came to the same conclusion. In Psalm 62:1 he writes, "My soul finds rest in God alone; my salvation comes from him."

HIGHLIGHT

God made us for himself, and our hearts are restless until they rest in him.
—Adapted from Saint Augustine

SAVING

Why do you think people look to wealth for happiness? because people are very materialistic and find joy - or think they can find joy in THINGS!

Why is wealth ultimately "meaningless"?

Where do you search for fulfillment?

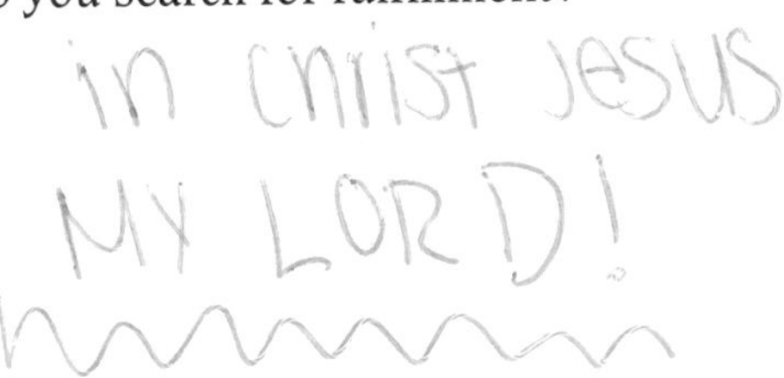

Pitfalls of Plan Making

The hot coffee burned Carla's throat as she swallowed, but she hardly noticed. After a week of sleepless nights, caffeine was the only thing getting her through the day.

Carla rubbed her eyes, which were dry for the first time since James left. "Choices have consequences," she remembered her minister saying. *No kidding,* Carla thought.

She had known deep down that she shouldn't marry James, a non-Christian, but she'd always wanted a husband and family, and James was so willing. Her plans for the future seemed full of promise when she accepted James's marriage proposal.

Carla took another sip of scalding coffee and pulled her bathrobe tightly around her. She imagined James drinking his morning coffee somewhere else with another woman, and her eyes were moist again.

DOWNLOAD BIBLE BYTE

Now listen, you who say, "Today or tomorrow we will go to this or that city, spend a year there, carry on business and make money." Why, you do not even know what will happen tomorrow. . . . Instead, you ought to say, "If it is the Lord's will, we will live and do this or that."

James 4:13–15

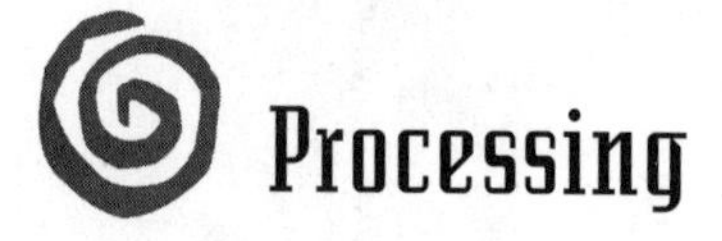

Processing

"What are you planning to do with your life?" Every teen faces this question sooner or later. As the junior high and high school years draw to a close, everyone wants to know what our plans are. Will we go to college? What kind of careers do we hope to have?

Planning ahead can be tricky business. On one hand, it's important to have goals. On the other, if we're not careful, we run the risk of putting our own desires ahead of God's will. If our plans aren't based on a desire to obey God, we're going to make unwise decisions that have consequences down the road. When Carla made plans, she let her own wants override what she knew was right, and as a result, she experienced disappointment and heartache.

We should pay attention to the advice offered in James 4:13–15. When we plan ahead, we should first consider what God wants from us. As you face the future, pray about your plans. Study the Bible to see how God has asked you to live, and ask him to guide you on *his* path for your life. Consult wise people around you and ask them lots of questions. Take advantage of all the resources the Lord has provided, including your own mind and your own conscience.

SAVING

What did Carla do wrong when she made plans for the future? She was only thinking of what she wanted, not what God wanted.

What are some possible reasons we fail to seek God before making plans? because we can be selfish

What are some specific ways you can make sure God is involved in planning your life's next step?

read the bible
Pray/talk to God.

The Ultimate Role Model

Janet dropped her backpack onto the school steps and stretched her shoulders. She'd been waiting over an hour and there was still no sign of her father.

"I'll remember," he'd promised that morning, throwing her a wave as he rushed out the door. But this was the third time in a month that he'd forgotten to pick her up after volleyball practice, and the routine was getting old.

As she sat down next to her backpack, Janet thought back to a time when she'd adored her father. But that was years ago, before he'd gotten too wrapped up in his job to remember that Janet or her mother existed. *I used to want to be just like him,* she remembered, frowning. These days, her father was the last person she wanted to imitate.

Fifteen minutes later, Janet rose as her father's brown sedan sped around the curve. His apologetic smile didn't make her feel any less forgotten. *Who am I supposed to look up to, Dad, if I can't look up to you?*

DOWNLOAD BIBLE BYTE

Be imitators of God, therefore, as dearly loved children.
Ephesians 5:1

Processing

Little kids always want to grow up to be like their parents, especially like their fathers. As children, many of us see our fathers as strong and wise, and we want to imitate them. As we mature, we come to realize Mom and Dad aren't perfect. That's when we start looking for other role models to imitate.

Being imitators of God is a tall order. Nevertheless, Matthew 5:48 commands us to "be perfect, therefore, as your heavenly Father is perfect." Obviously none of us can lead truly perfect lives because we're all sinners, but all the same we're commanded to imitate God, who is completely pure and holy. As his dearly loved children, we are to study his ways and do our best to grow into people who reflect his character.

What will our lives look like if God is our role model? Well, 1 John 4:16 says, "God is love. Whoever lives in love lives in God, and God in him." If we're true imitators of God, our lives will be characterized by the love our "role model" has shown us by adopting us as his dearly loved children.

HIGHLIGHT

God calls us his children for a reason. As his offspring, we carry his love in our veins, and he expects us to show it.

SAVING

How have some of your role models disappointed you? punishing me favoring others

In what ways does Ephesians 5:1 convict you?

since God is love we should love

What are some things you can do to imitate God in your friendships? love others respect others

“Dear God, Please . . .”

Janelle closed her bedroom door and pulled a notebook off her bookshelf. Lying down on the floor by the window, she opened the notebook and read through the week’s list of prayer requests. She’d written notes about her own needs as well as those of her family and friends. Bowing her head she asked God for help with each item on her list. As she prayed Janelle checked off each request. Fifteen minutes later she said, “Amen,” and rose from the floor.

As she replaced the notebook on the bookshelf, Janelle wondered at the unsettled feeling in her heart. Lately her prayer times hadn’t filled her with peace as they once had. Even though she felt like she was relying on God’s help more than ever, Janelle knew something was missing from her prayer life.

DOWNLOAD BIBLE BYTE

“This, then, is how you should pray: ‘Our Father in heaven, hallowed be your name, your kingdom come, your will be done on earth as it is in heaven. Give us today our daily bread.’”
Matthew 6:9–11

Processing

Sometimes we talk to God like he’s Santa Claus. We bow our heads, close our eyes, and pull out a mile-long list of requests. But Jesus taught us that prayer is more than an opportunity to go to God with needs and wants. It’s also a time to worship him and strengthen our relationship with him.

The prayer Jesus taught to his disciples didn’t start off with a request. It started with worship. Then, instead of stating desires, Jesus taught we should ask for God’s will to be done. The time for requests of

God's care and provision (our daily bread) comes only after expressions of praise and submission to God.

God wants us to ask him for things, but that's not the only reason for prayer. He wants us to spend time talking with him, sharing our thoughts, dreams, and sorrows. He wants us to thank and praise him for the things he's doing in our lives, and to seek his will for the future. Janelle felt something missing because she'd forgotten the many purposes of prayer. We should treat prayer as a conversation with our Creator, not as a turn on Santa's knee.

SAVING

When have you prayed *only* to give thanks and praise to God?

How do your prayers compare to Jesus' prayer in Matthew 6?

Why do you think God wants us to pray to him?

HIGHLIGHT

"We look upon prayer as a means of getting things for ourselves; the Bible's idea of prayer is that we may get to know God himself."
—Oswald Chambers, author of *My Utmost for His Highest*

Living Right

Living Right
Living Right

Forgiveness for the Humble

Nathan tried to hide his surprise when Jake Humphries walked through the door. Jake had never made an appearance at the after-school prayer meeting, and as one of Delaney High's more rebellious students, his presence was unexpected.

Well, it's not like I can ask him to leave, Nathan thought, so he shrugged off his surprise and continued praying.

God, thank you that I'm not like Jake, Nathan prayed silently. *I don't lead the kind of lifestyle he does. I go to church, I love my neighbors, and every day I try to follow your commandments.*

Beside Nathan, Jake covered his face in his hands, trying to hide his tears of remorse. *Forgive me, God,* he pleaded silently. *I'm so unworthy of anything good, especially from you, but please forgive my sins.*

DOWNLOAD BIBLE BYTE

"I tell you that this man, rather than the other, went home justified before God. For everyone who exalts himself will be humbled, and he who humbles himself will be exalted."
Luke 18:14

Processing

The story above is similar to a story Jesus told about a Pharisee and a tax collector. Tax collectors took money from the Jews and gave it to the Romans, the Jews' oppressors. Most of them went a step further and pocketed extra money for themselves. Needless to say, the Jews didn't think very highly of tax collectors. In Jesus' story a Pharisee prays, boasting that he isn't as sinful as the tax collector. The tax collector also prays, but instead of praising himself, he falls on his face and cries, "God, have mercy on me, a sinner" (Luke 18:13).

Jesus said the tax collector, not the Pharisee, went home justified before God. The tax collector's prayer showed humility. He was forgiven because he acknowledged his sinfulness and asked for God's mercy. The Pharisee's prayer showed conceit and self-righteousness. Rather than exalting God, he exalted himself. The Pharisee may have led what people thought to be a more holy life than the tax collector, but in God's eyes both men were sinners.

Humility is an important part of our relationship with God because it allows us to see our need for forgiveness. First Peter 5:5 says, "God opposes the proud, but gives grace to the humble." God forgives us when we admit our sinfulness and ask for his mercy. If we humble ourselves in this way, one day God will exalt us for our obedience to him.

SAVING

What was the difference between Nathan's and Jake's prayers?

Which character do you relate to more: Nathan or Jake?

Why was Jake's prayer more pleasing to God?

Get Up and Go

Gina set her empty plate on the coffee table and sighed as she reclined on the couch. It had been a long, tiring day, and she was ready to relax in front of the television for the rest of the night.

After flipping through a few channels, Gina found a soap opera she hadn't seen in weeks. Her parents had asked her not to watch it anymore, but they were out for the evening.

The show hadn't been on for long when Gina's conscience started nagging her. She knew she was disobeying her parents as well as filling her mind with trash. *Turn the TV off,* a voice inside told her. Gina tried to push the thought away and enjoy her freedom, but she couldn't get away from the simple command. *Turn it off.* Finally, Gina pushed the power button on the remote and the screen went blank.

DOWNLOAD BIBLE BYTE

The word of the Lord came to Jonah son of Amittai: "Go to the great city of Nineveh and preach against it, because its wickedness has come up before me." But Jonah ran away from the Lord and headed for Tarshish.
Jonah 1:1–3

Processing

Jonah didn't want to go to Nineveh, and he thought running away was the answer. But after being thrown off a ship, swallowed by a fish, and vomited onto dry land, he ended up preaching in Nineveh just as God had told him. Jonah learned obedience the hard way.

There were others in the Bible who weren't as slow to do what God asked. For example, Matthew 9:9 says, "[Jesus] saw a man named Matthew sitting at the tax collector's booth. 'Follow me,' he told him, and

Matthew got up and followed him." Matthew's obedience was immediate.

Why did Matthew and Jonah respond differently to God's calling? Perhaps it was more appealing for Matthew to follow Jesus than for Jonah to travel to Nineveh and preach to its wicked inhabitants. But if we only obey God when the task is easy, we're obeying our *own* wills, not God's. If God places a Nineveh-like task before you, remember Jonah's story. Running doesn't do any good, and it isn't pleasing to God. Rather than fighting him, we should get up and go, as Matthew did.

HIGHLIGHT

No matter what God sets before us, our obedience should be immediate and unconditional.

SAVING

Whom do you relate to more: Jonah or Matthew?

Why doesn't it make sense to run from God's calling?

Has God ever placed a Nineveh-like experience before you?

Rotten at the Core

won't be long," Dan mumbled as he stepped out of the car.

"Take your time," Heather said quietly. "We won't miss you."

When he slammed the door she turned to look at Carissa in the back seat. "I'm sorry," she said.

"Do you and your brother always fight?" Carissa asked.

"Seems like it," Heather said, and then, thoughtfully, "I wish I could be more like you, Carissa."

Her friend laughed.

"Why would you wish something like that?"

"Because you're so good. You'd never say the things I do."

"Heather," Carissa said, leaning forward to look her friend in the eye. "I might look good on the outside, but you don't see what I think and feel on the inside."

Processing

Have you ever known someone who appeared to live a perfect life? Some people always seem to have control of themselves. They never yell, curse, lose their tempers, or act inappropriately in any way. But does that mean these people are without sin?

According to the Bible, definitely not. Romans 3:23 says, "All have sinned and fall short of the glory of God." No human being is perfect, no matter how self-controlled they may be. The source of sin lies inside

DOWNLOAD BIBLE BYTE

"For from within, out of men's hearts, come evil thoughts, sexual immorality, theft, murder, adultery, greed, malice, deceit, lewdness, envy, slander, arrogance and folly. All these evils come from inside and make a man 'unclean.'"
Mark 7:21–23

us, not in our outward actions. We don't have to act out a sin to be guilty of it. For example, Matthew 5:28 says, "But I tell you that anyone who looks at a woman lustfully has already committed adultery with her in his heart."

We can't live sinless lives. Even when we keep our bodies in check, our minds go on sinning. We should strive to control our actions and our thoughts by focusing our minds on God. But remember, while we should try to eliminate sin from our lives, no one is perfect. We're all in need of God's grace and forgiveness.

HIGHLIGHT

We all need God, because regardless of how shiny we are on the outside, we're all rotten at the core.

SAVING

Have you ever known anyone who seemed to live without sin?

Why aren't we sinless when we control our outward actions?

What is the only cure for sin in our lives?

Tasty Talk

"Did you hear about Mel and Ryan?" Everyone around the cafeteria table turned their attention to Leah, who leaned forward and whispered, "They broke up over the weekend."

"What happened?" someone asked Leah, who began relating what she'd heard about the breakup.

Seated at the next table, Katie stiffened. As the other students gasped and giggled about the juicy details, she focused her attention on her macaroni and cheese and ate in silence.

"Wait until you hear what Ryan said about Mel!" Leah continued. As she went on, Katie pulled out her history notebook and tried to study for her quiz. But no matter how many times she reread her notes on the Civil War, she couldn't memorize anything. Leah's voice kept breaking her concentration with private information about Mel and Ryan.

DOWNLOAD BIBLE BYTE

The words of a gossip are like choice morsels; they go down to a man's inmost parts.
Proverbs 26:22

Processing

No matter which end of the talking we're on, gossip makes us feel important. When we gossip, people hang on everything we say. When we hear gossip, we feel special because someone is letting us in on privileged information. Even when we're not comfortable participating in gossip, like Katie, it's hard to resist. That's why words of a gossip are called "choice morsels." They're appealing to all who speak or hear them.

Regardless of how gossip makes the gossipers feel, it can be extremely hurtful and harmful to others. Proverbs 26:20 says, "Without wood a fire goes out; without gossip a quarrel dies down." Gossip fuels conflict because it often involves betrayal and deception. Sometimes friendships split up over the betrayal of a confidence. False rumors can ruin the reputation of an innocent person. To put it simply, gossip lies at the root of many painful situations.

Ephesians 4:29 tells us, "Do not let any unwholesome talk come out of your mouths, but only what is helpful for building others up according to their needs, that it may benefit those who listen." When we're involved in conversations about other people, we should consider our motivations for sharing or listening to information. Are our words spoken out of love and concern for another's well-being, or out of a selfish desire to be a part of tasty talk?

HIGHLIGHT

"Gossip is a sort of smoke that comes from the dirty tobacco-pipes of those who diffuse it; it proves nothing but the bad taste of the smoker."
—George Eliot, English novelist

SAVING

How would you respond in Katie's situation?

Why is it so hard to resist gossip?

Has gossip ever caused problems in the relationships in your life?

A Time to Pray

Todd leaned forward over the steering wheel, squinting to see through frost on his windshield. The mountain road ahead of him was shrouded in darkness, the falling snow so thick his headlights couldn't find the road behind a curtain of white. Cranking up the defroster Todd tried to relax. He knew this road. The steep decline coming up around the bend was sure to be slick in this weather.

Seconds later, Todd hunched over the wheel again as he eased his car down the hill. Testing the brakes, Todd discovered there was no traction. He held his breath as the car picked up speed, sliding dangerously to the right, where the road dropped off into a black abyss. Slamming his foot on the brake, Todd squeezed his eyes shut and whispered desperately, "God, help me!" As quickly as the words escaped him, the car stabilized on the roadside, and Todd opened his eyes and breathed a prayer of thanks.

DOWNLOAD BIBLE BYTE

One of those days Jesus went out to a mountainside to pray, and spent the night praying to God.

Luke 6:12

Processing

Prayer isn't something Christians always *want* to do. Unfortunately, few people jump straight from bed to their knees in the morning, eager to spend quality time with God. To many of us, prayer can feel more like a chore than the awesome privilege it really is.

Prayer is intimidating when we worry too much about how we pray instead of why we pray. For example, the verse above tells us Jesus spent hours talking to his Father in private, as he often did (Matthew 14:23; 26:36–44). But does that mean our prayers have to last for hours? Plenty of free time and a place to be alone are elements of a good prayer time, but they're not requirements. God doesn't care about length or location as much as he cares about the attitude and motives behind our prayers.

Consider Todd's prayer. It wasn't long, and it wasn't uttered in a quiet, peaceful place, but God still answered it. Todd's prayer was an earnest cry for help. Even though Todd was in an emergency situation, his prayer attitude wasn't any different from what ours should be. He was seeking God, and that's what prayer is all about.

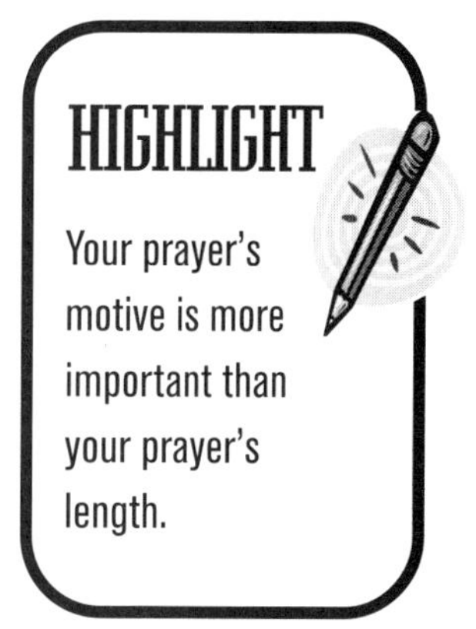

SAVING

Why did Jesus spend so much time in prayer?

How would you define a good time of prayer?

What are the motives behind your prayer times?

Discipline down the Road

Ted yawned as he dragged himself out of bed at 5:30 A.M. for his early morning jog. The predawn air was crisp as he started running. He drew in a deep breath, and the autumn smells reminded him of the previous fall when he'd started his morning running routine. Back then Ted hadn't been able to reach the end of his street without stopping for a breather. The memory brought a smile to his face, and he increased his speed, relishing the healthy burn in his leg muscles. *Five miles will go fast today,* he decided.

The year of training hadn't been easy. Every morning was a struggle for Ted, especially since he loved sleeping in. But if he missed even a few days, he always suffered the next time he ran. Ted had to force himself out of bed and onto the street every day, sacrificing an extra hour of sleep. It wasn't fun, but now that he could see the results, Ted knew every sleepless morning had been worth it.

DOWNLOAD BIBLE BYTE

No discipline seems pleasant at the time, but painful. Later on, however, it produces a harvest of righteousness and peace for those who have been trained by it.
Hebrews 12:11

Processing

A lot of people think of discipline as what parents do to misbehaving children, but it's more than that. Discipline isn't always a rebuke for inappropriate behavior. It is also what prevents us from sinning. The writer of Hebrews refers to discipline as a form of training. Discipline of the will strengthens our ability to resist temptation and live godly lives.

Let's compare discipline to athletic training. Athletes train their bodies for years. Their training is intentional, repetitive, and requires sacrifice of foods and pleasures that might hinder the athlete's progress. The training is painful, but if the athletes stop training, they'll backslide into poorer health and physical condition. If they continue, eventually their bodies will become healthy and strong, and all the hard work will be worth it.

Like physical discipline, discipline of the will requires intention, repetition, and sacrifice. We have to choose to resist temptations, and we have to make that choice on a daily basis. We also have to give up pleasures that lead us into sin or prevent us from growing closer to God. Discipline may be painful, but if we stick to it, the results will more than make up for our extensive training.

> **HIGHLIGHT**
>
> "You have to pay the price—but if you do you can only win."
> —Frank Leahy, former football coach for Notre Dame

SAVING

What areas of your life could use more discipline?

What are three characteristics of effective discipline?

What attitude should we have about discipline?

Risk Taking for Peacemaking

John rushed to the noise and commotion. A circle had formed in the hallway around Terra and Audrey, who were yelling obscenities at one another.

"I'll kill you!" Terra said.

In one motion, Terra took a step forward and shoved Audrey against the lockers behind her. The back of Audrey's head crashed hard against the metal, and she fell to the floor.

Terra grabbed a fistful of Audrey's hair and was about to repeat the act.

"Don't!" yelled John, elbowing his way through the circle of onlookers. Terra let go of Audrey's hair and looked at who it was.

"Butt out," Terra said.

"No. Please. Don't," John repeated, crouching down to touch Audrey's shoulder.

DOWNLOAD BIBLE BYTE

"Blessed are the peacemakers, for they will be called sons of God."
Matthew 5:9

Processing

The Jews of Jesus' day longed for God to free them from their Roman oppressors and to establish his kingdom. The disciples were waiting for Messiah, Jesus, to initiate a military battle with the Roman Empire. They wanted Jesus to show the Romans who was boss. But Jesus had different ideas. He said the way to freedom was to be a peacemaker. In the four gospels Jesus says "peace" twenty-one times.

Peacemaking is not easy. John, for example, risked a lot to help Audrey. He risked the ridicule of those who were enjoying the fight, and he risked getting his own head slammed against the lockers. Jesus risked a lot, too. The Jews wanted a military leader. If Jesus didn't give them what they wanted, he ran the risk of getting crucified, which is exactly what happened.

So, how do we do it? Where do we find the strength and courage necessary to confront and resist violence? Jesus gave us the answer when he said, "You will receive power when the Holy Spirit comes on you" (Acts 1:8). It is the Holy Spirit who gives us the power we need to be peacemakers. All we have to do is trust God and do the right thing. God will take care of us one way or another.

> **HIGHLIGHT**
>
> "The only thing necessary for the triumph of evil is for good men to do nothing."
> —Edmund Burke, British statesman and orator

SAVING

How was what Jesus wanted different from what the other Jews wanted?

What are the risks involved when we choose to be peacemakers?

On whom should Christians rely for the power to be peacemakers?

The Insider

"Nate, how'd that scratch get on my car?"

Nate turned away from his computer to see his father standing in the bedroom doorway. "It happened when I was at the mall, Dad. When I came out it was already there." The lie rolled off Nate's tongue just as he had practiced it.

"Why didn't you tell me earlier, son?"

"I thought you'd be mad," he said, relieved when his father shook his head.

"It's not your fault, Nate. But tell me next time, okay?" Nate nodded and turned back to his computer. The lie had worked, but his heart beat rapidly and beads of sweat formed on his forehead.

DOWNLOAD BIBLE BYTE

"And I will ask the Father, and he will give you another Counselor to be with you forever— the Spirit of truth." John 14:16–17

Processing

When Jesus told his disciples he'd be leaving them, they were devastated. After being with Jesus day and night, witnessing his miracles and hearing his teaching, they couldn't stand being without him. But Jesus promised that once he left they'd receive a new Counselor, the Holy Spirit.

The Father, the Son (Jesus), and the Holy Spirit make up the Holy Trinity. Although they're individual beings, they're all part of the same God. Jesus told his disciples, "Anyone who has seen me has seen the Father" (John 14:9). Jesus came from God, just as the Holy Spirit comes from God. Unlike Jesus, the Holy Spirit can't be seen or touched. It doesn't have a physical body, but dwells inside the Christian. First Corinthians 6:19 says, "Your body is a temple of the Holy Spirit, who is in you, whom you have received from God."

Every Christian receives the Holy Spirit. We're told the Holy Spirit guides us, convicts us of right and wrong, and teaches us the truth of God (John 15:5–15). Nate felt convicted for lying because the Holy Spirit was working inside him. Although conviction is uncomfortable, the Holy Spirit is a wonderful gift. It helps us obey God and experience his love, righteousness, and power during our lives.

HIGHLIGHT

The Insider is an honest friend—it tells us when we're messing up, but never abandons us when we do.

SAVING

When have you felt the conviction of the Holy Spirit?

How else does the Spirit work in you?

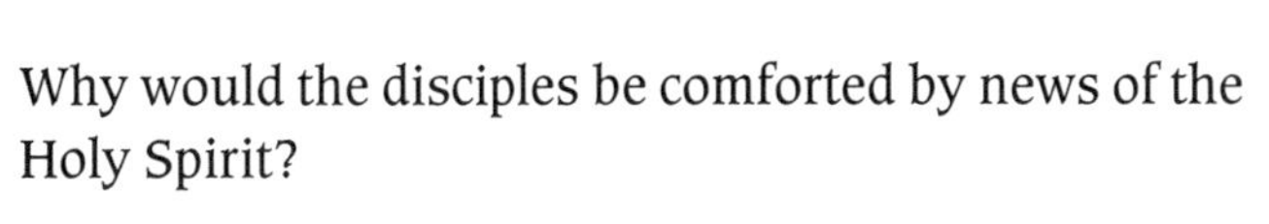

Why would the disciples be comforted by news of the Holy Spirit?

A Pig with a Nose Ring

Rachel groaned inwardly when she saw Jackie's car pull up in front of her house. Before opening the door for her latest guest, Rachel noticed unpleasant expressions on many of her friends' faces. No one wanted Jackie around, but asking her to leave was out of the question.

"Come on in, Jackie," Rachel said.

"Thanks," Jackie replied, following Rachel into the kitchen. "Wow, this house is tiny!" she said. "You must feel like a sardine living here." Rachel cringed at how loudly Jackie spoke and tried to ignore the rude comment. She offered Jackie a tray of cookies hoping a full mouth would keep the girl quiet.

"Oh, gross!" Jackie said after taking a bite. "These are terrible, Rach. What did you put in them?" Losing her patience, Rachel slammed the cookie tray down on the table and faced Jackie.

"What's the matter with you!" she yelled. "Why do you always have to be so rude!" For a moment Jackie was shocked into silence. But then she just shrugged her shoulders and smiled smugly.

"I just tell it like it is," she said. "If you can't take honesty, that's your problem."

DOWNLOAD BIBLE BYTE

"I, wisdom, dwell together with prudence; I possess knowledge and discretion."
Proverbs 8:12

Processing

Jackie was proud of her ability to "tell it like it is," but her bluntness was anything but admirable. Jackie's comments were hurtful, and they caused many people to turn against her. But if Jackie was only being honest, why were people so offended?

Jackie lacked discretion. Discretion is the ability to do and say the right thing in the right way at the right time. Discretion is important because it shows people who we are beneath the surface. Matthew 12:34 says, "For out of the overflow of the heart the mouth speaks." Indiscreet words are a sign of a selfish heart because they show people we don't consider the feelings of others. Jackie claimed she was just being honest, but because she failed to speak out of love her honesty only made people dislike her.

Proverbs 11:22 is a striking statement about indiscretion: "Like a gold ring in a pig's snout is a beautiful woman who shows no discretion." On the outside I might be as beautiful and delicate as a gold ring, but if my actions and words aren't discreet, people won't look at the ring. They'll look at the pig I am.

HIGHLIGHT

"People who are brutally honest get more satisfaction out of the brutality than out of the honesty."
—Richard J. Needham, Canadian journalist

SAVING

Do you know anyone like Jackie?

How can we be honest without being indiscreet?

Why is discretion important?

Letting the Light In

"You'd look great in this white dress," Debby said, pointing to a page in her magazine. Jen leaned over to take a look, laughing when she saw the photo.

"Yeah, right," she said. "With my hips I'd look like a marshmallow in that thing."

"You would not," Debby protested, as she studied the model in the magazine. The woman's face was framed by rich auburn curls, which were stunning against the white dress. Debby wound a strand of her own dirty blond hair around a finger and sighed.

"Hey," Jen said, interrupting Debby's thoughts. "This ad says I can lose weight by taking a shower! Can you believe that?"

Debby smiled but continued contemplating her limp hair. Jen fell silent again as she reread the advertisement. *Anything's worth a try*, she thought as she lifted the magazine to look at her thighs. "I hate the way I look," she said quietly. She looked at Debby, but her friend was still focused on the woman in the white dress.

DOWNLOAD BIBLE BYTE

"The eye is the lamp of the body. If your eyes are good, your whole body will be full of light. But if your eyes are bad, your whole body will be full of darkness."
Matthew 6:22-23

Processing

This study's Bible Byte is about the relationship between the things we look at and the way we live. What we look at enters us. Whatever our eyes focus on fills our hearts and minds and influences the kind of life we lead.

Put simply, the things we *watch* tend to be the things we *want*. Debby and Jen focused on physical beauty, so they wanted more than anything to perfect their bodies and look like magazine models. In the same way, if our eyes focus on wealth, we'll shape our lives around earning money and gaining earthly possessions. If our eyes focus on God and his will for us, holiness and obedience to his Word will take root in our lives.

It's tempting and easy to focus on the things of this world like money, beauty, and pleasure, but we can choose to deny those temptations and focus our eyes on God. We can focus our eyes on him by reading his Word and spending time in prayer. At times it might be hard to keep our focus, but if we *watch* God long enough, we'll *want* the things he wants for us.

HIGHLIGHT

Your eyes are the door to your heart. Be careful whom you allow to enter.

SAVING

What do you choose to focus on?

Why does what we watch affect us so strongly?

What should we focus on?

Repeat Offenders

As soon as Rodney was alone in the locker room, he slapped his hand against his forehead in frustration. "When will you ever learn?" he asked himself angrily.

His conversation with Jeremy replayed in his mind. The boys had been discussing their parents' salaries. When Jeremy asked how much Rodney's dad brought home every year, Rodney had named a high figure. He'd lied. Truth be told, Rodney's dad had just taken a pay cut. But Jeremy was always bragging about money, and Rodney couldn't stand to let him gloat. He knew the salary he'd made up was more than Jeremy's dad made.

But he had still told a lie. Rodney beat his hand against his forehead again. *Why can't you just tell the truth?* he asked himself. Lying was his weakness. Every time Rodney swore he'd never do it again, he found himself right back here—full of regret and shame.

Processing

When it comes to obeying God, do you ever feel like you have a learning disability? A lot of Christians make the same mistakes over and over again. Just when we think we've learned our lesson, we screw up all over again. We want to grow as Christians, but will we ever reach maturity?

DOWNLOAD BIBLE BYTE

You need someone to teach you the elementary truths of God's word all over again. You need milk, not solid food! . . . But solid food is for the mature, who by constant use have trained themselves to distinguish good from evil.
Hebrews 5:12, 14

Hebrews reminds us that spiritual maturity doesn't come overnight. Mature Christians have learned to do the right thing after years of training. They've studied the "solid food" of God's Word and constantly used their knowledge to grow. First Peter 2:2 says, "Like newborn babies, crave pure spiritual milk, so that by it you may grow up in your salvation." The Bible feeds our desire to grow as Christians. Its words nourish and strengthen us as we strive to please God.

Don't be frustrated if you're a slow learner like Rodney. Maturity takes time, but it *will* come. Philippians 1:6 promises, "He who began a good work in you will carry it on to completion." When you fall, let God set you on your feet again, and then keep trying. God's not finished with you yet!

HIGHLIGHT

God always finishes what he's started, and he's started something in you.

SAVING

What are some lessons you've had a hard time learning?

Why do we make the same mistakes over and over again?

How can we become mature Christians?

Tenants of the Temple

"You're sure you don't want to try one?" Mark asked, offering his cigarettes to Susan.

"I don't smoke," she replied, shaking her head. Mark tucked the pack into his front pocket.

"I know you don't smoke. I just don't understand why you won't try one."

"I don't see any reason to try something that isn't good for me, especially when it's something addictive." Susan sighed as he lit his cigarette, wishing her friend had never started smoking.

"Are you saying you're not even curious?" he mumbled out of the corner of his mouth, pocketing the lighter. "Aren't you tempted to try one and see what it's like?"

"I am a little curious," she admitted.

"So try one," Mark insisted, offering her his lit cigarette. "It's *your* body."

"No," Susan said, pushing his hand away. "Actually, it's not my body."

DOWNLOAD BIBLE BYTE

Do you not know that your body is a temple of the Holy Spirit, who is in you, whom you have received from God? You are not your own; you were bought at a price. Therefore honor God with your body.

1 Corinthians 6:19–20

Processing

When Paul wrote to the Corinthian church, he was addressing the issue of sexual immorality. But his message can also be applied to harmful practices like smoking and drug or alcohol abuse.

Throughout history, the temple was a holy, clean place set apart for worshiping God. Jesus drove merchants out of the temple in Jerusalem because they were misusing it by turning it into a marketplace. He rebuked them, saying, "Is it not written: 'My house will be called a house of prayer for all nations'? But you have made it 'a den of robbers'" (Mark 11:17).

Just like the temple, our bodies are meant to be God's dwelling place. Because of Jesus' death and our acceptance of God's forgiveness, we belong to him. Like Susan, we should treat our bodies as though we're tenants in someone else's building. By abstaining from sexual immorality, smoking, drugs, and other harmful practices, we obey the command of Romans 12:1: "Offer your bodies as living sacrifices, holy and pleasing to God—this is your spiritual act of worship."

HIGHLIGHT

Take care of your body as you would take care of another's property. Your Landlord doesn't want to see his temple misused.

SAVING

How does thinking of yourself as God's property affect your lifestyle?

How have you seen people suffer from abusing their bodies?

What are some ways you can enjoy being God's temple?

Abolishing Anxiety

Amy drummed her fingers across a page of her biology textbook, her other hand poised with a highlighter inches above the glossy paper. She'd been reading the same paragraph about photosynthesis for fifteen minutes and still hadn't run the marker over a single sentence. *Why does plant food production have to be so complicated*, she wondered, wishing once again she'd taken chemistry instead.

Dropping the highlighter into her lap, Amy fixed her eyes on the phone. *Melissa should be back from shopping now,* she thought. A chat with her best friend would be a welcome distraction from the fruitless studying, but Amy knew she had to keep reading if she wanted to pass tomorrow's quiz. *But I'll never be ready,* she fumed inwardly, dropping her head back against a cushion. Her anxiety grew as she thought of all the pages she had left to read before morning. *God, help me pass . . .* she began, then shook her head. *Never mind, Lord,* she prayed, *you've got better things to do.*

DOWNLOAD BIBLE BYTE

Do not be anxious about anything, but in everything, by prayer and petition, with thanksgiving, present your requests to God. And the peace of God, which transcends all understanding, will guard your hearts and your minds in Christ Jesus.

Philippians 4:6–7

Processing

Money, grades, relationships . . . you name it, we're probably worried about it. How often do you have all the money you need, the highest grades you can earn, and relationships without any tension or insecurity whatsoever? Rarely does life hand us everything on a platter, and when things don't go the way we'd like, our first tendency is to become anxious.

We're supposed give *every* worry to God, a concept that's not always easy to remember. If a family is rationing food and doesn't have the cash for a trip to the supermarket, prayer seems like the logical way to go. But in Amy's case the anxiety stemmed from studying for a quiz she didn't think she could pass. She believed her situation was too trivial to bring before God.

That's not what the Bible tells us. First Peter 5:7 says, "Cast *all* your anxiety on him because he cares for you" (italics added). God has proclaimed his love for us and invites us to share everything with him. If that means praying, "God, give me understanding so I can pass my biology quiz," so be it. He's the Almighty God, and he's listening to us.

SAVING

What "trivial" worries do you hold back from God?

Why do you think God wants us to give him *all* our worries?

What does God give us in exchange for our anxiety?

What's My Motivation?

Selena drummed her fingers against the steering wheel, her eyes on the Marcott's front door. She'd been parked across the street for an hour contemplating her next move. Beside her was an envelope containing every dollar she'd earned over the summer. Upon hearing about the Marcott's financial troubles, Selena had decided to give away her savings. Surprisingly, the choice to part with the money had been easier than the decision she now faced.

Should Selena walk to the Marcott's front door and hand them the money, or sneak to their mailbox and make an anonymous donation? She wanted to do it in person. It would be rewarding to hear a thank you, and the family was sure to tell others about her generosity.

What's my motivation? she asked herself.

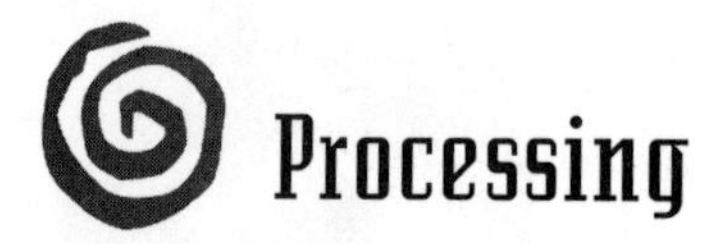

Processing

In Jesus' day the Pharisees were considered righteous men. They obeyed Jewish laws perfectly, always praying, fasting, and giving to the poor. But Jesus saw behind the false holiness of the Pharisees. He called them hypocrites (Matthew 6:5), claiming their motives weren't to serve God, but to serve themselves. The Pharisees gave money in public so they'd be praised for their generosity. When they prayed, they stood on street corners in view of everyone.

DOWNLOAD BIBLE BYTE

"Be careful not to do your 'acts of righteousness' before men, to be seen by them. If you do, you will have no reward from your Father in heaven."
Matthew 6:1

We all want approval. There's nothing wrong with this unless it becomes a selfish motivation. The Pharisees acted under the pretense of holiness when all they really wanted was respect and praise. In other words, they lied.

We don't start out with an intention to deceive people, but it's easy to be fooled by our own motives. As long as we're doing the right thing, we don't necessarily think about *why* we're doing it.

Proverbs 16:2 says, "All a man's ways seem innocent to him, but motives are weighed by the Lord." When you do "acts of righteousness," search the motives in your heart as Selena did. The purest motives come from love for God and others.

SAVING

How often is praise a motivation for your actions?

What are some other motives for acting holy?

What should our motives be?

Blessed for Obedience

Shannon blinked back tears as Trent and the others laughed at her. "Shannon, I can't believe you're scared of a child's game."

"It's not a child's game. It's a Ouija board," she insisted, but her trembling voice only made them laugh louder. *Maybe I should just play with them*, she thought, but Shannon believed the Ouija board was dangerous. It was supposed to communicate with spirits, and she knew it was wrong to communicate with any spirit other than God.

"Come on, Shannon. Don't be a baby." Trent patted the carpet, inviting her to sit down. "We're just going to play around with it for a few minutes." Shannon looked around the room, meeting every pair of eyes focused on her. She could see her refusal to go with the flow would have lasting consequences.

"No," she finally said. She turned away and grabbed her coat, fighting tears once again as laughter chased her from the house.

DOWNLOAD BIBLE BYTE

Now Joseph was well-built and handsome, and after a while his master's wife took notice of Joseph and said, "Come to bed with me!" But he refused.

Genesis 39:6–8

Processing

Joseph knew he was putting himself in danger when he refused to sleep with Potiphar's wife. As a slave Joseph could have been killed for his disobedience. Then, instead of telling her husband the truth of what happened, Potiphar's wife claimed Joseph had tried to take advantage of her. Potiphar believed the lie and had Joseph thrown into prison.

Joseph's situation seemed unfair. He didn't do anything wrong, so why should he have to suffer? Some of us face the same question when we're punished for choosing to obey God. When people urge us to do something wrong, it's often easier to give in than to face ridicule or anger.

In Matthew 5:11 Jesus says, "Blessed are you when people insult you, persecute you and falsely say all kinds of evil against you because of me." Blessed? Shannon didn't feel blessed when she was ridiculed. And Joseph probably didn't feel blessed when he found himself in jail because of someone else's lie. But eventually Joseph ended up in charge of all of Egypt. God always rewards our obedience to him. If you're ever unfairly punished for following God's commands, remember Jesus' words: "Rejoice and be glad, because great is your reward in heaven" (Matthew 5:12).

HIGHLIGHT

When people make fun of you for following Christ, remember Joseph's story. There are blessings in your future.

SAVING

How have you been persecuted for your religious beliefs?

What were the short-term and long-term results of Joseph's obedience to God?

How might God bless you for obeying him?

Gravel in a Gift Box

Trina ran her finger over the sweater's soft sleeve as her eyes scanned the store. One sales associate was helping a customer near the back. The other was talking quietly on the phone, clearly not paying attention to anyone. Trina glanced toward the exit and saw Holly motioning to her. *Do it now,* she was mouthing, a daring smile on her face.

In one quick movement Trina pulled the sweater from its hanger and tucked it into her backpack. When no one seemed to notice, she strolled casually from the store and raced with Holly to the safety of their car.

"I can't believe you did it!" Holly said, grabbing the backpack from Trina. She pulled the sweater out and laughed. "This is going to look great on you!"

Trina smiled, but as they drove away she felt her excitement fading. She shook her head and tried to swallow the guilt, but her throat was tight and dry. *What have I done?* She ran her fingers over the sweater again, but this time its softness only grated at her conscience. *If only I could go back and undo this . . .*

DOWNLOAD BIBLE BYTE

Food gained by fraud tastes sweet to a man, but he ends up with a mouth full of gravel.
Proverbs 20:17

Processing

Sin can be exhilarating. If it wasn't, why would we do it? There's something about breaking the rules that gets our blood pumping. But the excitement is short-lived, and in its path comes a wave of regret.

Satan is a master of deception. He started with Eve, making the forbidden fruit look sweet. But her sin had lasting consequences for all humankind. Satan tries to do the same thing to us. He wraps sin up in a pretty package and places it on our doorstep, hoping we'll be deceived by its enticing appearance. It's only after we've pulled the wrapping off that we recognize the rottenness of what's inside.

Trina wanted the sweater and the thrill of taking it. She got all she wanted and more. Her guilt and shame were like a mouthful of gravel—grating, choking, and nauseating. She wanted to turn back the clock and undo her sin, but she couldn't. She'd been deceived by the master of lies. When Satan leaves a package at your door, don't be fooled by it's attractive exterior. Whatever he's hidden beneath the wrapping is sure to bring you nothing but regret.

SAVING

Why did Trina steal the sweater?

What kinds of "packages" does Satan leave on your doorstep?

How is sin like a "mouthful of gravel"?

Rock Solid

ut it's my business partner's fault!" Ray shouted into the phone. "He's the one who stole from my company!"

"Mr. Sherman, the bank doesn't care who's to blame," the loan collector replied. "You're bankrupt, and we want the money you owe us."

"Well, I'm sorry," Ray said. "I don't have that kind of cash."

"You have vacation homes, expensive vehicles, and a large estate outside the city," the man argued.

"What?" Ray whispered, sinking into a chair. The phone shook in his hand as reality began to sink in. "You're going to take everything I have? I've worked for years to build this life, and you're taking it away?"

"I'm sorry, Mr. Sherman. Your business is gone, along with our money. We have no other choice."

After telling his disciples about the house with a foundation on rock, Jesus told them about a second man who heard Jesus' words but didn't put them into practice. Jesus compared this second man to a builder who constructed his house on the sand. When the rains and wind came, his house "fell with a great crash" (Matthew 7:27). Its foundation wasn't strong enough to hold the house together through the storms.

On the outside both houses might have looked identical. But when the storms came, everything was

DOWNLOAD BIBLE BYTE

"Therefore everyone who hears these words of mine and puts them into practice is like a wise man who built his house on the rock. The rain came down, the streams rose, and the winds blew and beat against that house; yet it did not fall, because it had its foundation on the rock."
Matthew 7:24–25

stripped away to reveal the foundation, which is where a house's strength comes from. The same is true of people. Our foundations are on whatever we base our strength, hope, and worth. Hopefully Ray Sherman did not base his life on wealth, because if so, he just found out the hard way that money can disappear in the blink of an eye. Anyone can build a confident outward appearance, but when life's storms hit, we're only as strong as our foundation.

By listening to God's Word and obeying his commands, we establish a firm foundation. Psalm 62:2 says, "He alone is my rock and my salvation; he is my fortress, I will never be shaken." All the money, power, and success in the world can't build a foundation as solid as God. He is eternal. God will remain forever, but all other foundations will weaken and erode like sand.

HIGHLIGHT

Worldly riches shift like the sand, but a foundation built on God is rock solid.

SAVING

What are some things on which people build their foundations?

What is your foundation built on?

How is the strength of a foundation tested?

A Matter of the Mind

Richard drummed his fingers on the kitchen countertop and looked at the clock. His favorite television show, *Justice*, would be on in ten minutes, but Richard wasn't going to watch it. *Justice* was a police drama that had grown increasingly violent in recent seasons. Although Richard still enjoyed the show, for a long time it left him feeling angry and aggressive every Tuesday night.

But not this time, he determined. At eight o'clock he went to his bedroom and grabbed his Bible. Though he'd been a Christian for years, Richard hadn't spent much time studying Scripture. He wanted to replace the negative influence of *Justice* with something positive, and he knew there was nothing more positive than the Bible.

Richard didn't stop reading until almost 9:30. He was amazed at the excitement he felt after reading through Luke's account of Jesus' life. The stories about Christ were interesting and uplifting. As Richard lay in bed that night, instead of wondering what he'd missed on *Justice,* his mind turned to the verses he'd read.

DOWNLOAD BIBLE BYTE

Finally, brothers, whatever is true, whatever is noble, whatever is right, whatever is pure, whatever is lovely, whatever is admirable—if anything is excellent or praiseworthy—think about such things.
Philippians 4:8

Processing

What does it mean to live a righteous life? The Bible gives us instructions on how to conduct ourselves in a way that pleases God. We know we're supposed to show love, generosity, humility, and kindness. But there's more to righteous living than outward appearances.

Even when our actions seem loving or humble, sometimes our minds are filled with angry or prideful thoughts. In attempting to live righteous lives, our thoughts are often the hardest thing to regulate. Romans 8:6 tells us, "the mind of sinful man is death." How can we tame the evil thoughts that plague our minds?

Paul advised Christians to focus on worthwhile things, so that our minds would be full of purity instead of ugliness. Richard discovered the truth behind Paul's teaching when he changed his television habits. If we fill our minds with negative images, we think negative thoughts. But if we fill our minds with "excellent or praiseworthy" things, our thoughts will be noble and admirable.

HIGHLIGHT

Only when our righteous actions are accompanied by righteous thoughts can we begin to live righteous lives.

SAVING

How can we tame our sinful thoughts?

What are some "excellent or praiseworthy" things to fill our minds with?

What are some ways entertainment affects your ability to live righteously?

To Drink, Or Not to Drink

Mitch looked up from his computer as headlights flashed through his bedroom window. Pulling back the curtain, he watched as his dad's car drifted to a halt with one wheel in the flower bed. The door fell open and his father emerged, staggering as he moved toward the house.

Mitch rose to lock his bedroom door, then grabbed his portable phone. He could hear muffled voices downstairs. He held his breath and listened as his father's voice grew louder. Even through the floor, Mitch could understand his foul words. Suddenly a crash vibrated through the house, followed by the sobs of Mitch's mother. Mitch shuddered and clenched his fist as he dialed a friend's number.

"Jim, it's Mitch," he said. "I can't make it tonight."

"Your dad again?" Jim asked.

"I'm never touching alcohol," Mitch said. "I don't know why anyone would."

"Well, not everyone is like your dad," Jim said. "But I understand how you feel."

DOWNLOAD BIBLE BYTE

Who has needless bruises? Who has bloodshot eyes? Those who linger over wine. . . . Do not gaze at wine when it is red, when it sparkles in the cup, when it goes down smoothly! In the end it bites like a snake and poisons like a viper.

Proverbs 23:29–32

Processing

Alcohol causes a lot of controversy among Christians. Some people believe drinking is okay as long as it's done in moderation, while others think it's always wrong. One thing we know for sure is that the Bible does warn us not to drink too much. Ephesians 5:18 says, "Do not get drunk on wine, which leads to debauchery."

We're supposed to care for our bodies as if they were someone else's property, God's property. First Corinthians 6:19-20 says, "You are not your own; you were bought at a price. Therefore honor God with your body." Drunkenness doesn't honor God because it harms our bodies and "leads to debauchery." In other words, it makes us more vulnerable to temptation and sin.

The issue of alcohol is something all Christians must think about. Drinking before you are of age is always wrong because it is illegal. Before you are old enough to drink, it is a good idea to think about what God wants you to do about alcohol. Be sure to pray, study the Bible's teaching, and don't be afraid to ask questions of other believers.

HIGHLIGHT

"One reason I don't drink is that I want to know when I'm having a good time."
—Nancy Astor, former member of British parliament

SAVING

How do Christians you know feel about drinking?

What are some of the different motivations for drinking?

What are two ways that drunkenness can be destructive?

Fearfully and Wonderfully Made

Will watched from the empty bleachers as the football team practiced for an upcoming game. Notebook in hand, he scribbled down his observations about the new starting quarterback. As the school newspaper's sports reporter, Will was expected to inform his fellow fans about the team's chances in Saturday's game.

Wish I were out there, he thought. He imagined the announcer's voice booming through the speaker system: *Another touchdown by number 35 . . . Will Horst.* He heard the applause and saw himself dancing in the end zone. *Yeah, right,* he thought. *I'm barely coordinated enough to walk straight, let alone run and catch a football.*

"Hey, Will."

A little startled, Will looked to his right at one of his classmates. "Hey, Ben. What's up?"

"I was wondering," Ben said. "Who's gonna win this Saturday? Your predictions are always right on."

DOWNLOAD BIBLE BYTE

My frame was not hidden from you when I was made in the secret place. When I was woven together in the depths of the earth, your eyes saw my unformed body. All the days ordained for me were written in your book before one of them came to be.
Psalm 139:15–16

Processing

In Psalm 139 we learn God arranged every cell in our bodies exactly as he desired. If a perfect and holy God created us, why do we often feel like failures?

Feelings of inadequacy come when we focus on our weaknesses instead of our strengths. If you feel inadequate in physically demanding activities, turn your attention to other areas of your life. God has gifted every one of us. We just need to find out what our gifts are and learn how and when to use them. Will didn't have the coordination to be a running back, but his understanding of the game and his way with words made him a great sports reporter.

Sometimes it's difficult not to be jealous of the gifts of others, but we're wiser to be content with whom God made us and to focus on developing the gifts God has graciously given to us.

HIGHLIGHT

To criticize the way you were made is to criticize the workmanship of God.

SAVING

What is wrong with being jealous of other people's gifts?

What are your gifts?

How can you develop the gifts God gave you?

Willpower over Emotion

Danielle sat at her kitchen table watching the stove clock. She'd have to leave soon to make it to church on time for the food drive.

Danielle stirred her spoon around in her forgotten cereal and slumped in her chair. *Maybe I won't go,* she thought.

When she promised to help with the food drive, she thought it would be fun. But since then she'd run into problems with everything. Her parents were fighting, school wasn't going well, and after last night's fight she didn't know if she still had a boyfriend.

Danielle looked at the clock again. If she didn't leave now, she'd be late. *I shouldn't help if I feel this way*, she reasoned, but she knew the excuse was weak. *But you promised,* she told herself.

Mustering her willpower, Danielle forced herself up and grabbed her car keys.

DOWNLOAD BIBLE BYTE

"Whether it is favorable or unfavorable, we will obey the Lord our God."

Jeremiah 42:6

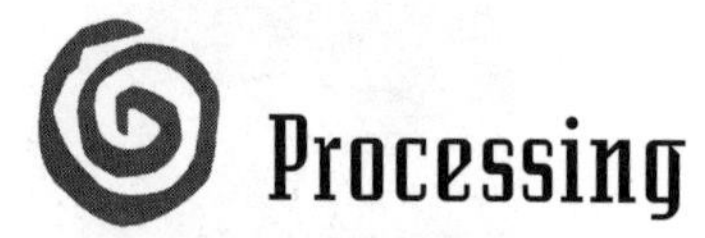

Processing

Our society places a lot of emphasis on emotions. "Follow your heart," we're told. The problem is, the whims of our hearts change on a daily basis, especially during the teen years when life if full of transition. If we can't trust our chaotic emotions, what do we turn to as a basis for our behavior?

When our emotions are running rampant, we have to will ourselves to behave and think as God has instructed us. There are few things harder in this life than acting in opposition to our emotions, but at times we have to do just that in order to obey God. Danielle is a perfect example of will over emotion. She knew backing out of her commitment would be wrong. She had to use her willpower to keep the promise.

Our behavior should never be based on how we feel, because emotions change constantly. They're affected by what we think, do, and even what we don't do. They're affected by food and physical activity. We can't depend on our emotions to help us behave appropriately. We have to know the Bible, and we have to exercise our wills to obey what the Bible says.

HIGHLIGHT

"The discipline of emotions is the training of responses."
—Elisabeth Elliot, well-known Christian author

SAVING

How often do your emotions determine your behavior?

Why is it unwise to be influenced too much by our emotions?

How do we avoid being controlled by our emotions?

On the Outside Looking In

Nell flinched when Ben slapped a flyer down on her cafeteria table.

"Party at my place Friday." He grinned mischievously at Nell and her lunch companions. "My parents are out of town."

Brian grabbed the flyer as Ben spread the word.

"Says it's going to be 'the party to end all parties.'" Brian said. "You guys going?"

"Ben's parties are awesome!" Sandy said.

Several heads nodded in agreement. Nell kept her eyes down as everyone talked about the party. She'd heard about Ben's parties. There'd be alcohol in the backyard, drugs in the basement, and sex in the bedrooms. The title of last Sunday's sermon flashed in her mind: "Saying No to the World."

"Nell, you going?" someone asked. Nell looked up, nervously.

"I don't know," she blurted. "I mean, maybe I'll go."

DOWNLOAD BIBLE BYTE

Do not let your heart envy sinners, but always be zealous for the fear of the Lord. There is surely a future hope for you, and your hope will not be cut off.
Proverbs 23:17–18

Processing

As Christians, sometimes we feel like we're on the outside looking in. While our peers party all night long, we're told to live to please God. That means giving up the carefree lifestyle that seems to bring everyone else so much pleasure. But even though we know about the sins involved in "the party scene," sometimes we're like Nell—wishing we could join the crowd.

It's hard to hang back and watch while other teens indulge in the world's "fun." Instead of envying them, we're supposed to be passionate about God's laws. That's tough to do when his laws are the reason we don't party with our peers.

The pleasures of the world are attractive because they're in front of us right now and because they *are* pleasurable, at least for a time. God's pleasures, on the other hand, often require a waiting period. The world can give us pleasure *now*, but the world doesn't tell us that its pleasures often lead to horrible pain in the future. Unlike the fading pleasures of the world, the pleasures God offers last forever. We may have to wait for the joy and pleasure he'll give us, but the wait is worth it because in the end there will be no pain—only joy, forever and ever.

HIGHLIGHT

Pleasure without a future hope is a poor substitute for God's eternal promises.

SAVING

What are some of the things you envy about non-Christians?

Why are the world's pleasures attractive?

The pleasure of God differs from the pleasure of the world in what ways?

Working in Paradise

Tonya kneaded the sore muscles in her lower back and moaned. "I hate this job," she said, knowing the same words had come from her mouth many times before. Untying her apron, she tossed it over the back of a chair and slowly lowered herself onto the floor where she could stretch her aching legs.

"I share your hatred," Dennis said with a smile. He was quiet for a moment as he counted his tips from the evening, then he turned toward Tonya. "But I need the money too bad to quit."

"Me, too," she agreed. She pulled out her tips, but the wad of bills was disappointingly small. "Can you imagine living somewhere where we wouldn't have to work?" she asked. Dennis laughed.

"Sorry, Tonya, but paradise doesn't exist."

"I know," Tonya said. "But if this was a perfect world, I'll bet there wouldn't be any such thing as working."

DOWNLOAD BIBLE BYTE

There is nothing better for a man than to enjoy his work, because that is his lot.
Ecclesiastes 3:22

Processing

People complain more about their jobs than just about anything else in life. It's easier to think of work as a punishment rather than a blessing. After all, work takes up our time and energy when we'd rather be doing other things. Isn't that why we get paid for it?

As with many things, God's view of work is a little different than our own. Tonya was wrong to think a perfect world wouldn't include work. Contrary to what we might imagine, God didn't create work as a punishment for Adam and Eve's sin. Genesis 2:15 says, "The Lord God took the man and put him in the Garden of Eden to work it and take care of it." God created work back when the world was perfect! He intended for us to take pleasure in our labor!

I know what you're thinking: "Does this mean we have to *enjoy* working?" That's especially hard for us to do when we're students (we don't even get paid for what we do!). But schoolwork is work, just the same. As far as enjoying it, we should try. After all, God wouldn't have created it if he didn't think it was a good idea.

> **HIGHLIGHT**
>
> "Work is not man's punishment. It is his reward and his strength, his glory and his pleasure."
> —George Sand, French romantic writer

SAVING

What are some reasons people complain about their jobs?

Why do you think God created work?

What is your attitude toward working?

Good, But Not Good Enough

Hannah's lungs burned as she neared the top of the hill. Her body was screaming for rest, but Hannah ignored the slamming of her heart and the pain in her legs as she pushed forward with even more speed. *You're never going to get into shape if you quit now*, she told herself.

Hannah had been running for months, but no matter how strong her legs became or how much her speed improved, she was never satisfied. The same was true of everything else in Hannah's life. When she tried her best in school, she never thought her grades were high enough. And whenever she competed in regional voice competitions, she was never satisfied with her placement. She was driven by one thought that stayed with her day and night: *I'm not good enough. I have to be better.*

DOWNLOAD BIBLE BYTE

"You will not surely die," the serpent said to the woman. "For God knows that when you eat of it your eyes will be opened, and you will be like God, knowing good and evil."

Genesis 3:4–5

Processing

All the insecurities we have about our personalities, bodies, and abilities can be traced back to the Garden of Eden. Ever since Eve ate the forbidden fruit, humans have struggled with feelings of inadequacy. Satan told Eve eating the fruit would make her like God, implying that she wasn't good enough the way God had created her. Eve chose to believe Satan's lie, and her choice sent the rest of humankind on a frantic search for self-worth.

Eve failed to realize God's creation was perfect just the way he'd made it. Genesis 1:31 says after God finished creating the earth and its inhabitants he "saw all that he had made, and it was very good." Unlike Eve, who was created without sin, people today are born sinners. We have shortcomings because of our sinfulness, but there is a difference between fighting sin and being plagued by the kind of insecurity Hannah felt.

In Psalm 139:13–14 David writes, "For you created my inmost being; you knit me together in my mother's womb. I praise you because I am fearfully and wonderfully made." God formed our bodies and filled us with talent, humor, and intelligence. He created us exactly the way he wanted us. Rather than beating ourselves up for what we perceive are inadequacies, we should praise him for his work and rejoice in the gifts he's given us.

HIGHLIGHT

God accepts us because he loves us, not because of anything we do for ourselves.

SAVING

Have you ever felt like Hannah?

Why do we struggle with feelings of inadequacy?

What does the Bible tell us about ourselves?

Old Habits Die Hard

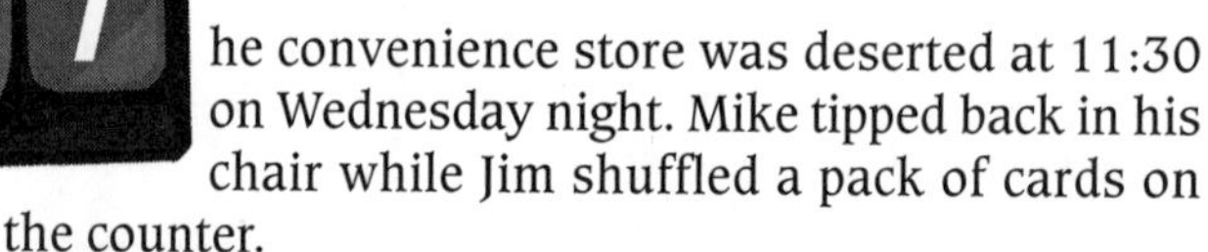

The convenience store was deserted at 11:30 on Wednesday night. Mike tipped back in his chair while Jim shuffled a pack of cards on the counter.

"How'd that church thing go last night?" Jim asked.

"It was good, actually," Mike said, smiling at Jim's expression.

"Oh, boy," Jim said. "Don't tell me you're one of those Christians now."

"Actually, yeah, I . . ." Mike trailed off when the phone rang.

Jim answered, then hung up. "Wrong number," he explained. Looking around, he clapped his hands together. "Okay, the store's dead, and I'm hungry. It's ice cream time." He walked toward the freezer. "Want your usual flavor?"

Mike didn't answer.

"What's wrong?" Jim asked.

Mike's mouth watered as he thought about his favorite mint chocolate chip ice cream. "I can't," he said. "It's stealing."

"But we've been doing this for months," Jim said. "Don't you want it?"

"Of course," Mike said. "But what I want isn't always what God wants. I should obey his will, not my own."

DOWNLOAD BIBLE BYTE

For the sinful nature desires what is contrary to the Spirit, and the Spirit what is contrary to the sinful nature. They are in conflict with each other, so that you do not do what you want.
Galatians 5:17

Processing

There is a war going on inside each of us. The Holy Spirit, which hates evil and desires to obey God, is fighting against the sinful nature, which allows us to be tempted into sin. As long as we live in our earthly bodies, these contradicting forces will battle for control of our thoughts and actions.

This war is evident in Mike's life. When he became a Christian, the Holy Spirit allowed Mike to see the sinfulness of his old ways. Even though he hated the things he'd done, Mike was still tempted by the sinful nature to repeat his past sins. His story echoes Paul's words in Romans 7:15: "I do not understand what I do. For what I want to do I do not do, but what I hate I do."

Resisting the sinful nature requires a conscious choice to follow God and remember the battle is already won. The death and resurrection of Christ defeated sin, and because of his victory we are "dead to sin but alive to God in Christ Jesus" (Romans 6:11). That doesn't mean we won't struggle with sin during our earthly lives, but we can be encouraged knowing that God will help us resist the temptations before us.

HIGHLIGHT

"It is easier to prevent ill habits than to break them."
—Thomas Fuller, English clergyman

SAVING

What are some bad habits you have a hard time conquering?

Why was Mike tempted to steal?

How can we overcome the sinful nature?

Overcoming Life's Obstacles

Overcoming Life's Obstacles
Overcoming Life's Obstacles

Chain Reaction

The gravestone had weathered since Andy's last visit. The winter storms and summer rains had turned the shiny slate to a cloudy gray, and orange and red leaves were beginning to pile around the base. Andy brushed the leaves away and laid a bouquet of daisies against the stone, tracing his finger along the engraved letters that spelled "Marie Susan Clark."

When his girlfriend died, Andy didn't know how to live. It was like part of his heart had died with her, and for months he went through life feeling half empty. Each morning for months he begged God for the strength to get out of bed, brush his teeth, put on his clothes, and make it through the day.

It had been a year now, and though Andy still missed Marie, the emptiness he'd felt before was gone. The void inside had been filled by God, his Comforter. As Andy knelt by the graveside, he found himself smiling with joy, knowing that at that moment Marie was safe in the arms of that same Comforter.

DOWNLOAD BIBLE BYTE

Perseverance must finish its work so that you may be mature and complete, not lacking anything.
James 1:4

Processing

Perseverance is about persisting in difficult situations when we want nothing more than to escape. Andy persevered after Marie's death by getting out of bed and living his life. Others persevere by supporting an unappreciative friend or finishing homework for a hard class.

Why does God allow us to go through difficult things that require perseverance? Part of the answer is in the verse above. Perseverance brings about changes inside us that wouldn't occur if our lives were always easy. The apostle Paul expresses a positive attitude about perseverance in Romans 5:3–4 saying, "We also *rejoice* in our sufferings, because we know that suffering produces perseverance; perseverance, character; and character, hope" (italics added).

Perseverance is the first step in a chain reaction. Andy learned through his suffering to rely on God for strength and fulfillment. Whatever trials we face, we can rest in the knowledge that God will not only help us persevere, he will bring us closer to himself in the process.

HIGHLIGHT

When you don't have the strength to put one foot in front of the other, God will carry you.

SAVING

How did Andy change through his suffering and perseverance?

How do you persevere in your daily life?

What good comes from trials?

Change of Plans

Jared leaned against the gymnasium wall and quietly observed his classmates as they donned their blue and white graduation gowns. He spotted Ben Starke, the class president, pacing nervously in front of the bleachers. *Probably rehearsing his speech*, Jared thought.

During his junior year Jared had wanted nothing more than to be the class president, but he'd lost the election to Ben. The loss was even harder to take the next year when Jared lost the senior class election to the same person.

Looking back, Jared was thankful that his plans to be the class president hadn't worked out. During his junior and senior years he'd learned a lot about himself as he explored other interests and met new people. Sure, he would have been a good class president, but Jared knew he would have missed out on a lot if he'd won those elections.

DOWNLOAD BIBLE BYTE

Many are the plans in a man's heart, but it is the Lord's purpose that prevails.
Proverbs 19:21

Processing

The words above were written by Solomon, king of Israel. Solomon knew what it was like to see God's purpose prevail. As a young king, Solomon's plans were simple—he asked only for wisdom to rule Israel. God gave him wisdom, but also riches, honor, and a long life (1 Kings 3:10–14).

God dealt a little differently with Jared than he did with Solomon, but he gave them each more than they asked for. Jared didn't know he had other interests, and he didn't ask for new friends, but God chose to give him both.

Sometimes we look back at the past and feel relief that things didn't work out as we'd planned. Unlike our plans, Psalm 33:11 tells us "the plans of the Lord stand firm forever, the purposes of his heart through all generations." God doesn't ever have to change his mind because he can see the past, present, and the future all at once. Next time your plans fail, remember that God has a purpose in mind, and if you trust in him you'll get more than you bargained for.

HIGHLIGHT

Trust in God's purposes. He never has to resort to Plan B.

SAVING

How do you feel when God changes your plans?

How has God blessed you by allowing your plans to fail?

Why should we trust that God's plans are better than our plans?

A New Kind of Peace

"Peaceful?" Jason raised an eyebrow of skepticism. "You say you're feeling peaceful?"

"Yeah," Tom insisted, nodding emphatically. "That's the perfect word for it."

"I don't get it. Your parents just told you they're getting a divorce, Janice broke up with you two weeks ago, we've got a killer exam in Calculus tomorrow, and you're feeling 'peaceful'?" Jason shook his head. "I don't get it, man."

Tom shrugged at Jason, thinking about what his friend had said. It *was* a little hard to believe Tom could have peace when his life seemed to be falling apart. His parents had always seemed so happy, so the news of their divorce was a shock. And losing Janice was a blow he hadn't seen coming. Tomorrow's exam? Well, his chances of passing didn't look too good. So why *was* he feeling so peaceful?

"It's because of God," Tom finally said. "I don't get it either, Jay. I just know it's because of him."

DOWNLOAD BIBLE BYTE

"Peace I leave with you; my peace I give you. I do not give to you as the world gives. Do not let your hearts be troubled and do not be afraid."
John 14:27

Processing

Jesus spoke the words of this Bible Byte to his disciples shortly before his arrest and crucifixion. How could this man, knowing he was about to suffer a cruel death, speak of having peace? Peace, as humans usually think of it, involves freedom from conflict and trial. A "peaceful" life is one of comfort, harmony with others, and safety from danger. But Jesus wasn't talking about that kind of peace.

Jesus' crucifixion and death certainly weren't peaceful. But as he looked ahead to the pain waiting in his path, Jesus wasn't overcome by fear. His peace wasn't dependent on whether or not everything was going right in his life. Jesus' peace was from confidence in God instead of circumstances.

Isaiah 26:3 says, "You will keep in perfect peace him whose mind is steadfast, because he trusts in you." A steadfast mind is focused intently on God, undistracted by life's ups and downs. Philippians 4:7 tells us that God's peace "transcends all understanding." Tom didn't understand everything about his peaceful attitude, but he knew where it came from. Fasten your mind on God. He'll give you a peace that far exceeds human understanding.

SAVING

When do you feel most peaceful?

Why did Jesus feel peace?

Where does your peace come from?

Defeating Depression

"Sarah, can I come in?" Lynn knocked softly on the bedroom door. She hadn't seen Sarah in weeks, but she'd heard about her friend's depression.

There wasn't a response to her knock, but Lynn opened the door anyway. Sarah was sitting on her bed looking out the window. She didn't turn as Lynn stepped into the room. "Sarah?"

The room looked and smelled awful. Clothes lay in piles all over the floor. Dirty dishes covered the dresser and desk. Lynn swallowed hard as she studied Sarah's matted hair and rumpled T-shirt. She was pale and thin, and when she finally looked at Lynn there wasn't a trace of emotion in her blue eyes.

"Hello," she finally said. Her voice came out cracked and quiet, as though she hadn't used it in weeks. Lynn sat on the bed and tried to smile.

"How are you?" she asked. Lynn looked away and blinked slowly.

"They say I'm depressed," she said. "But I just feel . . ." She never finished the sentence, but went on staring out at the summer sky.

Download Bible Byte

I have been deprived of peace; I have forgotten what prosperity is. . . . I remember my affliction and my wandering, the bitterness and the gall. I well remember them, and my soul is downcast within me.
Lamentations 3:17, 19–20

Processing

The writer of Lamentations was depressed after witnessing the death and destruction of the Chaldeans' assault on Jerusalem. Unfortunately, depression is familiar to many of us. The words "my soul is downcast within me" are a perfect description of depression—it feels as though the deepest, most central part of us is broken and hopeless. Sarah's depression may seem severe, but it's a devastating reality for many.

Depression is a strong emotion, but there is a way to escape its grasp. We have to look past our feelings and focus on the facts. That's how the writer of Lamentations pulled himself out of depression. He said, "Yet this I call to mind and therefore I have hope: Because of the Lord's great love we are not consumed, for his compassions never fail" (Lamentations 3:21–22).

God's faithfulness, power, and love for us are *facts*. They don't change no matter how hopeless and depressed we feel. If we turn to him in our anguish, God *will* help us. Psalm 34:18 says, "The Lord is close to the brokenhearted and saves those who are crushed in spirit." Those words are true. Cling to the facts, and depression will lose its hold on you.

HIGHLIGHT

Depression comes and goes, but God's love for us never fades.

SAVING

Have you ever experienced severe depression?

Why do you think depression is such a strong emotion?

How can we escape depression?

Peace through Acceptance

"I lost my job today," Brian's mother said. She sat across from him at the kitchen table with her hands folded casually before her.

"What?" Brian cried out. "What happened?"

"The company is downsizing," his mother replied calmly. "My position is gone."

"What are we going to do?" Brian asked, his anxiety mixed with irritation as he studied his mother. "Why aren't you upset? This is terrible!"

"It's difficult," she agreed. "But it's also a blessing." When Brian frowned, she reached over to squeeze his hand. "Honey, I've been uncomfortable with the company's policies for a while now, but I refused to leave because we needed the money."

"But we still need the money," Brian insisted. "How is getting fired a blessing?"

"God knew I wouldn't take myself away from the job," his mother said. "So he took the job away from me. Now I can move on to a job that is more pleasing to God and more satisfying to me."

Brian pulled his hand away and rose to pace the kitchen. If his mother wanted to thank God for doing this to them, he'd let her. But he wasn't about to thank him for it.

DOWNLOAD BIBLE BYTE

"I am the Lord's servant," Mary answered. "May it be to me as you have said." Then the angel left her. Luke 1:38

Processing

Mary had plenty of reasons to be upset when an angel told her she'd be having a baby. She was an unmarried teenage girl, and the pregnancy could destroy her reputation. Would her family and friends believe the child she carried was a miracle, or would they think she was lying? Would her fiancé Joseph still marry her, or would he think she'd been unfaithful to him?

Mary could have been angry or fearful at the angel's news, but instead she chose to rejoice. She recognized how blessed she was to be the mother of the Messiah.

HIGHLIGHT

Peace is gained by surrendering to God, not by fighting him.

Brian's mother and Mary felt peace because they trusted God. Both women believed God's will is perfect and shouldn't be questioned. The Bible promises us the same peace when we place our trust in God. "You will keep in perfect peace him whose mind is steadfast, because he trusts in you" (Isaiah 26:3).

Brian refused to accept something that was beyond his control, and instead of peace, he felt anger and bitterness. But no matter what comes into our lives, we are his servants and must submit to his plans for us. If we're willing to accept God's will and trust his wisdom, he'll give us the same peace Mary felt.

SAVING

Why was Brian's reaction different than his mother's?

Why did Mary rejoice at the angel's news?

How should we respond to unexpected or unwanted events in our lives?

Beating the Unbeatable

Paul paced outside the library as he waited for the school board meeting to adjourn. He'd asked permission for the choir to sing religious songs at the spring concert, but Paul wasn't hopeful that the board would say yes. Earlier in the year they'd banned school prayer and denied requests for a student Bible study.

Why am I still here? Paul wondered. After losing his notes and stumbling nervously through his argument, Paul was sure his presentation had been unconvincing.

Paul looked up as the vice principal walked through the library doors. The man smiled and reached out to shake Paul's hand. "Congratulations, Paul," he said. "Your request has been granted." Paul was speechless. Smiling finally, he prayed, *thank you, God*. Paul knew the victory had nothing to do with his talent for public speaking.

DOWNLOAD BIBLE BYTE

The Lord said to Gideon, "You have too many men for me to deliver Midian into their hands. In order that Israel may not boast against me that her own strength has saved her, announce now to the people, 'Anyone who trembles with fear may turn back. . . .'" So twenty-two thousand men left, while ten thousand remained.

Judges 7:2–3

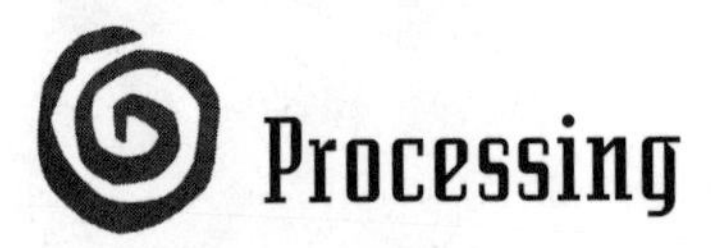

Processing

God didn't stop diminishing Gideon's army until there were only three hundred men remaining. Considering the size of the Midianite army, Gideon must have wondered what God was thinking. The opposing army's camels "could no more be counted than the sand on the seashore" (Judges 7:12). How would three hundred men triumph over such a powerful enemy?

First Samuel 14:6 says, "Nothing can hinder the Lord from saving, whether by many or by few." God can rise above any obstacle to accomplish his purposes. He reduced the size of Gideon's army to prove that point. Gideon and his men were victorious against the Midianites, but if they'd gone into battle with thousands of men, they would have boasted about their own strength. By minimizing their forces, God showed them his power in the midst of their weakness.

Sometimes God allows us to face seemingly unbeatable odds for the same reason. If our lives were always easy, we'd think we were responsible for our own success. We'd see ourselves as the source of our own strength and happiness, rather than realizing that all goodness comes from God. Philippians 4:13 says, "I can do everything through him who gives me strength." When you feel like the odds are stacked against you, remember that God's strength always beats the odds.

HIGHLIGHT

"Unbeatable odds" don't exist when you're relying on God's power.

SAVING

Why does God let you face "unbeatable" odds?

When have you been most aware of God's power?

How have you responded to unbeatable odds in the past?

An Attitude of Faith

Brandon waved from his riding lawn mower as Macy Turner jogged past his house. Smiling brightly, Macy waved back and continued down the sidewalk. *Amazing,* Brandon thought, thinking of Macy's joyful smile. *How can she be so happy only weeks after losing her mother?*

When the news spread that Macy's mother had tragically died in a car wreck, Brandon had expected his friend to be crushed. But when he visited Macy a few days after the accident, he'd been amazed at her attitude.

"God is in control of everything, Brandon. Even this," she'd said, smiling even as the tears ran down her cheeks.

"But aren't you hurting? Aren't you even a little angry about all this?" Brandon had questioned.

"Of course I'm hurting," she'd said, wiping her cheeks. "But how can I be angry when I believe God has a reason for everything?"

"Macy, I can't believe how strong you are."

"No, I'm not strong," she'd said. "But I know Someone who is."

DOWNLOAD BIBLE BYTE

After they had been severely flogged, they were thrown into prison. . . . About midnight Paul and Silas were praying and singing hymns to God, and the other prisoners were listening to them.

Acts 16:23, 25

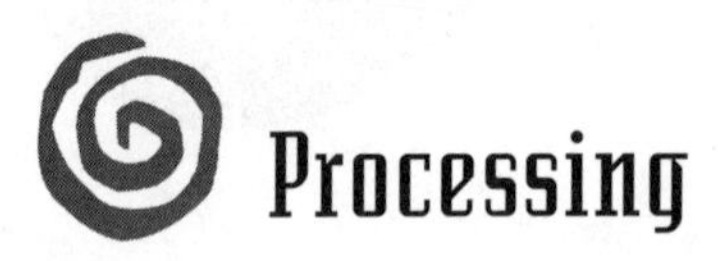

Processing

Paul and Silas weren't criminals who belonged in prison. They were imprisoned because the Romans were bigoted against their religious practices and Jewish background. Paul and Silas were beaten and thrown into prison without a trial or a legitimate reason for their suffering.

The amazing thing about this story is the faith of Paul and Silas. They didn't worry about what might happen to them or complain about the unfairness of their situation. After being stripped, beaten, and tossed into jail, they chose to worship God.

In Philippians 4:12–13 Paul writes, "I have learned the secret of being content in any and every situation . . . I can do everything through him who gives me strength." Paul and Silas had unshakable faith in God's power, and because of their faith they didn't complain or throw a pity party over their unjust imprisonment.

Life *isn't* fair, but Paul was right: we can do everything through God. Faith in his power and wisdom can give us the ability to do more than survive life's trials. It can allow us to praise him in the midst of our struggles just as Paul, Silas, and Macy did.

HIGHLIGHT

Having an attitude of faith means we trust God's eyes more than we trust our own.

SAVING

What is your typical way of reacting to trials in your life?

How does faith in God's power affect your view of suffering?

Decisions, Decisions . . .

Deena crushed a pillow over her head and pressed her face against the mattress. She didn't want to crawl out of her safe, warm bed and face her uncertain future. Today she would have to decide where to attend college. It was the biggest decision Deena had ever made, and after months of weighing her options she didn't even feel close to a decision.

Deena's mother wanted her to attend a nearby university and drive home for weekend visits, while her father encouraged her to go to his old college across the state. To top it off Deena's own desires were just as divided as her parents'. How was she supposed to make this decision?

As Deena hid beneath the pillow, fear gripped her. The choice she made about college would affect the rest of her life. What opportunities would she miss out on if she made the wrong decision?

DOWNLOAD BIBLE BYTE

"For I know the plans I have for you," declares the Lord, "plans to prosper you and not to harm you, plans to give you hope and a future."
Jeremiah 29:11

Processing

Deena wasn't the first person to shy away from making a big decision. Most of us are slow to choose between two paths that are almost identical, especially when our choice will have lasting consequences. There's nothing wrong with taking time to make decisions, unless our hesitation comes from fear. Is there any reason to be afraid of big decisions?

According to the verse above, no. As long as we're seeking God, we can't mess up God's perfect plans for our lives. That doesn't mean we will always make great decisions, but in the end God works everything out for our good (Romans 8:28). And if we sincerely seek his will in our decisions, he'll guide us to the best option.

Deena was frightened because she didn't have faith in God's sovereignty. She hadn't sought his will, and she believed her future was entirely in her own hands. But God is the overseer of our futures, and he can see our lives from beginning to end. Psalm 139:16 says, "All the days ordained for me were written in your book before one of them came to be." When you come to a crossroads, don't be frightened. Seek God's will and trust in him. Whatever path you choose, he'll always be leading you toward a future of hope.

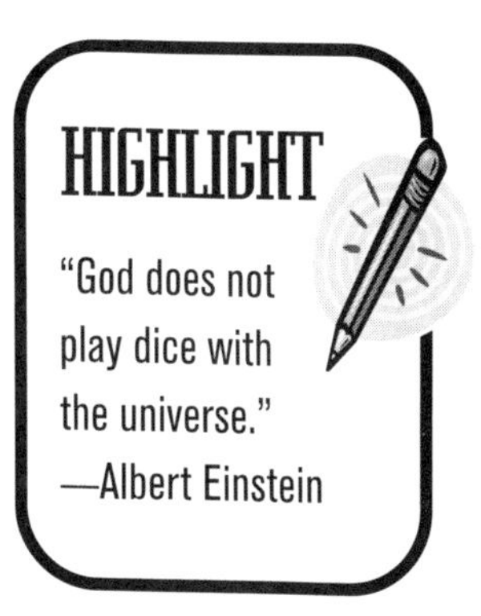

SAVING

What big decisions are you making right now?

What makes us anxious when we have to make decisions?

What is the key to ridding ourselves of this anxiety?

Rain before the Harvest

"No more video games until your grades go up."

"What!" Joel exclaimed. He dropped his fork on the plate and stared wide-eyed at his father.

"I'm sorry, Joel. But after my last meeting with your guidance counselor I'm really concerned about your schoolwork."

"But, Dad, I just bought my new PlayStation a month ago. You can't expect me to stop using it already."

"Yes, I can," his father said, his expression stern. "In the month since you bought that thing your grades have gone into a tailspin."

Joel sat back with a sigh of frustration. He could tell his father wasn't about to budge. "I don't see why you're doing this to me," he mumbled, already knowing what his father's response would be.

"You will, Joel. Give it some time, and eventually you'll understand."

DOWNLOAD BIBLE BYTE

My son, do not despise the Lord's discipline and do not resent his rebuke, because the Lord disciplines those he loves, as a father the son he delights in.
Proverbs 3:11–12

Processing

"If you don't eat your vegetables, you don't eat dessert," parents often insist. Many children end up sitting at the dinner table all night, thinking about how rotten life is. But parents force kids to eat nutritious food because they love them.

God, our heavenly Father, also disciplines us out of love. He doesn't ground us or take away TV privileges, but he does allow us to experience hardship. Through suffering we learn the lessons of life. Like little children around the dinner table, we usually can't understand the reason for our suffering when we're actually going through it. It's only when we've matured and grown in wisdom that we can appreciate the good that comes from suffering the consequences of bad decisions.

Hebrews 12:11 tells us our sufferings will result in a "harvest of righteousness and peace." But we don't have to wait for hindsight to accept and even be thankful for our suffering. Try to see suffering as a part of God's loving plan for your life, and you'll be reaping that harvest sooner than you think.

> **HIGHLIGHT**
>
> "Show me an orchestra that likes its conductor and I'll show you a lousy conductor."
> —Goddard Lieberson, former president of Columbia Records

SAVING

Why is discipline painful?

What is the motivation behind God's discipline?

How has discipline in your life brought about good results?

Living in the Rearview Mirror

Brad unbuckled his seatbelt and turned to his father.

"Why don't you stay for dinner?" he asked, but his father shook his head.

"Sorry, Brad," he said. "Your mom has a new husband now. I can't."

"Why not!" Brad yelled. "Why can't things be like they used to?" He fought tears as memories of family dinners played in his mind. His father reached over to squeeze his arm.

"Brad, I miss the happy times too. But don't forget that we weren't always happy." Brad pulled his arm away and sat back in his seat, refusing to think of the alcoholism that had torn them all apart. His father sighed. "Brad, I've been sober for almost a year. And you and I were never this close before I stopped drinking." Brad shook his head and reached for the door handle.

"I just want our family back," he mumbled.

DOWNLOAD BIBLE BYTE

"Forget the former things; do not dwell on the past. See, I am doing a new thing!"
Isaiah 43:18

Processing

In this verse, God is speaking to the Israelites, whom he rescued from slavery in Egypt long ago. When God says people shouldn't dwell on the past, he is referring to the time when he saved the Israelites and destroyed their Egyptian conquerors. The exodus, as the journey from Egypt is called, was indeed a miraculous event. God warns the Israelites, however, that if they focus too much on what he has already done, they will miss what he is doing in the present.

In this lesson's story Brad was so focused on what it was like when his parents were together that he failed to rejoice in the strides his father was making against alcoholism. Furthermore, Brad failed to see the improvement that had taken place in his relationship with his father. Imagine the joy he'd experience if he relinquished his grip on the past and seized instead the goodness of his new situation.

This Bible Byte reminds us that God never leaves us. He does not work in our lives for awhile and then desert us. He is *always* passionately working for our good. Whether we recognize that he is at work is our own choice.

When life gets hard, it's easy to turn our thoughts back to the "good old days." Some people might think about their childhood, while others remember being happy just last week. Either way, dwelling too much on the good of the past can blind us to the good of the present.

SAVING

What is good in your life right now?

What lessons are you learning from your present situation?

When does looking at the good of the past become a burden instead of a blessing?

Tried And True

Anthony entered the sanctuary when no one else was there, except Pastor Tim. The pastor stood behind the pulpit studying his sermon notes. Anthony was nervous about talking to the pastor, but he had to share his problem with someone.

Anthony had been dating Rebecca for two years. Even though they'd agreed to save sex for marriage, resisting the temptation was extremely difficult. Anthony had found himself pushing their physical relationship, always regretting his actions later.

But I can't talk to my pastor about this, he thought. *He'd never understand.* Pastor Tim was always levelheaded about everything. Anthony couldn't imagine the man struggling with sexual temptation when he was a teenager.

Anthony was also having a hard time praying about the problem. *God doesn't understand what this feels like,* he thought.

DOWNLOAD BIBLE BYTE

For we do not have a high priest who is unable to sympathize with our weaknesses, but we have one who has been tempted in every way, just as we are—yet was without sin.
Hebrews 4:15

Processing

A lot of people share Anthony's struggle. It's hard to believe pastors, priests, and other church leaders are tempted by sin like the rest of us. Some people seem so holy and pure that we see them as more than human. It's even harder to believe Jesus dealt with temptation during his time on earth. But Jesus, the "high priest," was tempted in every way.

Sometimes, because Jesus never sinned, we think resisting temptation was easy for him. But it's probably more accurate to say Jesus' struggles with temptation were worse than anything we can imagine. We give in to sin, but Jesus had to endure temptation at its worst and still remained sinless. That kind of battle must have been exhausting. Matthew 4:11 tells us after Satan tempted Jesus, "the devil left him, and angels came and attended him."

It should be comforting to us that Jesus knows better than anyone else how it feels to be tempted. His knowledge of temptation is far deeper than our own, so we should never hesitate to go to him with our weaknesses. Hebrews 4:16 says, "Let us then approach the throne of grace with confidence, so that we may receive mercy and find grace to help us in our time of need." He has overcome temptation, and through him we can find strength to resist sin.

HIGHLIGHT

Jesus was a man, and like all men he had to choose between sin and holiness. He chose holiness, and through him we can do the same.

SAVING

What common misconception was Anthony making about his pastor?

What temptations might Jesus have faced that you also struggle with?

Where does our ability to resist temptation come from?

An Ever-Present Help

The neighborhood was silent when Bethany tiptoed onto her back deck. She leaned against the railing and breathed in the still night air. It felt like the whole world was asleep, and Bethany's loneliness deepened. Her parents slept upstairs, unaware of her midnight wanderings. They had no idea she was lonely. No idea she felt frightened and friendless.

Looking up at the night sky, Bethany was reminded of her childhood years when she used to attend Sunday school. Her teacher had once said God created the moon and stars. But where was God now? Did he care about the world he'd created? Bethany thought of him watching her from somewhere beyond the galaxy. *But I need someone here*, she thought. *Someone to stand beside me, not watch me from far away.*

Processing

When Moses stepped down as leader of the Israelites, Joshua took his place. Moving on without Moses' trustworthy presence was probably scary for Joshua, but Moses reminded him of a presence far more powerful than his own. God's presence would be with Joshua and the Israelites as they crossed the Jordan River without Moses.

How often do we really think about God's presence? Many people imagine that God lives in heaven. It seemed to Bethany that God was far away. But

DOWNLOAD BIBLE BYTE

Then Moses summoned Joshua and said to him in the presence of all Israel, "Be strong and courageous. . . . The Lord himself goes before you and will be with you; he will never leave you nor forsake you. Do not be afraid; do not be discouraged."
Deuteronomy 31:7–8

who's to say God isn't sitting right beside you reading these very words?

Psalm 46:1 says, "God is our refuge and strength, an ever-present help in trouble." We might not be able to see or touch God, but that doesn't mean he's not here. God's presence is always with us, just as he was with Joshua. In fact, God isn't content to be just *near* us. He sent the Holy Spirit to dwell *inside* everyone who believes in Jesus (1 Corinthians 6:19). So when you feel frightened and alone, remember that God's presence can't get any closer, and he'll never leave you.

HIGHLIGHT

Though God's heavenly kingdom seems far away, his presence dwells inside your own heart.

SAVING

Where do you imagine God's presence to be?

Have you ever "felt" God's presence?

Why should God's presence give us strength and courage?

Don't Give Up

Frank ran a hand through his hair and sighed. No matter how many times he crunched the numbers, the calculator always told him the same thing—there wasn't enough money to keep the homeless shelter running.

Downstairs homeless men and women slept on cots. Many of them hadn't spent a night inside for weeks. Frank had opened the shelter because he believed God wanted him to. And now, in spite of his financial troubles, Frank still felt God wanted the shelter to stay open. "Lord, if this is your will, please provide the money," he prayed.

As Frank prepared for bed, his anxiety over the finances disappeared. He felt peace that lingered even when he awoke the next morning. When he looked through the day's mail, Frank discovered an anonymous check donated to the homeless shelter. Tears of gratitude to God sprang to his eyes as he realized the check would be enough to keep the shelter running for at least another month.

Processing

The walls around Jerusalem lay in ruins for almost a century and a half before Nehemiah tried to rebuild them. The task was overwhelming, but Nehemiah knew God wanted him to rebuild the walls. Even when he suffered the mocking of Sanballat, Nehemiah didn't give up. He trusted God to help him

DOWNLOAD BIBLE BYTE

When Sanballat heard that we were rebuilding the wall, . . . he ridiculed the Jews, and in the presence of his associates and the army of Samaria, he said, "What are those feeble Jews doing? . . . Can they bring the stones back to life from those heaps of rubble—burned as they are?"
Nehemiah 4:1–2

reconstruct the walls regardless of how impossible the job seemed.

Why didn't Nehemiah quit? His determination didn't come from pride or pressure from others as ours often does. He kept working because he wanted to serve God. Nehemiah's determination echoes the words of the Apostle Paul in 1 Corinthians 15:58: "Always give yourselves fully to the work of the Lord, because you know that your labor in the Lord is not in vain."

Frank's story is similar to that of Nehemiah, but rather than facing ridicule Frank struggled with finances. When we're working for God, all kinds of obstacles might pop up before us. But don't be discouraged. "Commit to the Lord whatever you do, and your plans will succeed" (Proverbs 16:3).

HIGHLIGHT

No matter how overwhelming the obstacles seem, when you're serving God, he won't let you down.

SAVING

Where did Nehemiah's determination come from?

When was the last time you got discouraged from doing God's work?

How can we avoid discouragement when serving God?

One Day at a Time

“What’s wrong, Neil? You look stressed,” Kyle said, sitting down across the table from his brother.

“I *am* stressed,” Neil replied, rubbing his hands over his face. He gestured to the papers spread out in front of him. “I’ve got this speech to give tomorrow and I’m really worried about it.”

“But I thought you were ready,” Kyle said. He’d been watching Neil prepare the speech for weeks. He’d assumed his brother would have it memorized by now.

“It’s not that,” Neil said. “I know it by heart, and I’ve practiced for hours. I guess I’m as ready as I’m going to get.”

“So what’s the problem?” Kyle asked, confused.

“I’m just worried,” Neil said. “I don’t know how it will go tomorrow.”

DOWNLOAD BIBLE BYTE

“Therefore do not worry about tomorrow, for tomorrow will worry about itself. Each day has enough trouble of its own.”
Matthew 6:34

Processing

Am I going to pass my test tomorrow? Will my team win the soccer tournament? How will my speech go? There are plenty of reasons to worry about tomorrow. Every day ends with unanswered questions and unresolved situations. How are we supposed to relax when tomorrow is on its way?

The Bible doesn’t say we should forget tomorrow exists and live as though today is the only reality. Common sense tells us to be aware of where our lives are headed, but worrying about things we can't control doesn't accomplish anything. As Matthew 6:27 says, "Who of you by worrying can add a single hour to his life?"

It sounds like Neil's problem wasn't lack of preparation. It was an excess of anxiety. He couldn't stop worrying about how he would do.

Yes, tomorrow is on its way, but rather than worrying about all the uncertainties of the future, we can focus on the present. Each day has its own trouble, so we should choose a course of action *today* that will help us to quit worrying about *tomorrow*. For example, instead of worrying about passing a test, we can sit down and study for it. Rather than worrying about a soccer tournament, we can go to bed early so we'll be rested for the game. Neil could have chosen to get his mind off his speech by watching a movie or reading a good book. As long as we're fulfilling our responsibilities for the present, there's no reason to be anxious about the future.

HIGHLIGHT

"He that fears not the future may enjoy the present."
—Thomas Fuller, English clergyman

SAVING

What kinds of things do you worry about?

What does worrying about the future do for us?

What should we do instead of worrying about the future?

Thy Will Be Done

Jeremy rose from the corner of his brother's hospital bed as a nurse entered the room. She smiled a greeting and went to work checking monitors and jotting notes on her chart. Jeremy remained silent, having seen the routine many times since Tim's accident.

"Do you think he'll ever wake up again?" Jeremy asked. The nurse smiled and pointed to a scribbled note on the chart.

"The doctor is hopeful," she said. When Jeremy didn't return her smile, she set the clipboard down and turned to him. "That doesn't help much, does it?" she asked.

"I can't stand this waiting," Jeremy said. "I feel so helpless."

"Have you tried praying?" the nurse asked softly. Jeremy shrugged and rubbed the back of his neck.

"I've spent hours in that prayer chapel," he said, motioning down the hall. "I begged for a miracle. I promised I'd do anything for God if he'd heal Tim."

"Have a seat, Jeremy," the nurse said, moving toward two chairs by the window. She waited until they were seated, then asked, "What if healing Tim isn't God's will?"

"I can't accept that," Jeremy said firmly.

"I know it's hard," the nurse said, "but if you're praying to God, don't you think it's time you started trusting him?"

DOWNLOAD BIBLE BYTE

"Father, if you are willing, take this cup from me; yet not my will, but yours be done."
Luke 22:42

Processing

When Jesus prayed the words in Luke 22, he knew that the time of his crucifixion was approaching. As he faced the coming days, Jesus' anguish was so great that the Bible tells us "his sweat was like drops of blood falling to the ground" (Luke 22:44).

Even in the midst of his distress, Jesus did not question God's goodness or wisdom. He could have been angry with God for allowing him to endure such unbearable pain or he could have taken matters into his own hands by running from his captors. Instead, Jesus asked that God's will be done, even if it meant he had to suffer and die.

God will never ask us to do exactly what Jesus did, but he may ask us to trust him through other kinds of painful experiences, like the one Jeremy went through. The next time you find yourself in a tough situation, follow Jesus' example.

HIGHLIGHT

"Acceptance of the will of God means relinquishment of our own. If our hands are full of our own plans, there isn't room to receive His."
—Elisabeth Elliot, well-known Christian author

SAVING

How did Jeremy and Jesus react differently to their circumstances?

What didn't Jesus do in his distress?

In hard times, do you pray more like Jeremy or Jesus?

Have a Healthy Heart

Kristen snapped off her television and pulled her bedspread tightly around her. *Why can't I feel better?* she wondered, thinking about her night of television viewing. Nursing a broken heart wasn't easy, but Kristen had been sure that losing herself in sitcoms would get her mind off her failed romance for one night.

Far from helping her escape, the hopeless world portrayed on television made her feel even more brokenhearted. As she drifted off to sleep, scenes from the night's episodes ran through her mind, leading her into deeper and deeper despair.

DOWNLOAD BIBLE BYTE

Above all else, guard your heart, for it is the wellspring of life.
Proverbs 4:23

Processing

Ever wonder why people think of the heart as the center of emotion? It doesn't make much sense when you consider the heart's bodily function. Our hearts pump blood through our veins and arteries, while our brains are where we actually decipher our feelings. Yet come Valentine's Day you won't find anyone doodling sketches of gray matter in their notebooks—you'll see little hearts with arrows through them.

Solomon wasn't thinking about the heart as a bodily organ when he wrote Proverbs 4:23. Rather he used the function of the physical heart as a metaphor. The heart is the "wellspring of life" in two ways. It provides life-giving nutrients to every part of the body by transporting blood, but it is also the center of our spiritual and emotional lives.

What does it mean to guard your heart? The answer is simple: Watch what you consume. Just as we put junk into our bloodstream by eating unhealthy food, we also put junk into our emotions by feeding on the world.

Instead of guarding her broken heart, Kristen filled up on junk that offered nothing of God's healing. Just like cholesterol or saturated fat can clog our arteries, the mental junk we consume can have a bad effect on our emotions. Guard your heart by filling it with knowledge of God. If you do, your life will be filled with love, goodness, and eternal life.

SAVING

What are some practical ways to guard your heart?

Why did Kristen feel more depressed after watching television?

Why did Solomon consider the heart to be such an influential part of us?

Releasing the Past

"What?" Jessica said, trying to hide her surprise at Tara's question.

"I said I was wondering if you'd like to be one of the youth group leaders next year."

"What do the other leaders think?" Jessica asked. She couldn't imagine them wanting her to be on the team. *I'm still a new Christian,* she thought. *They can't have already forgotten what I used to be.*

"They're all excited about it," Tara said, but Jessica just shook her head.

She'd joined the youth group less than a year ago. Until then she'd filled her life with men, drugs, and anything else that might fill the void inside. When nothing worked, she'd decided to look into God. A year later Jessica had finally found what she'd been searching for. *But I have such an awful past,* she reminded herself. How could she claim to be a youth group *leader* after the things she'd done?

"Thanks, Tara, but I don't think it's a good idea," she finally said, and walked away before Tara could respond.

DOWNLOAD BIBLE BYTE

Therefore, if anyone is in Christ, he is a new creation; the old has gone, the new has come!
2 Corinthians 5:17

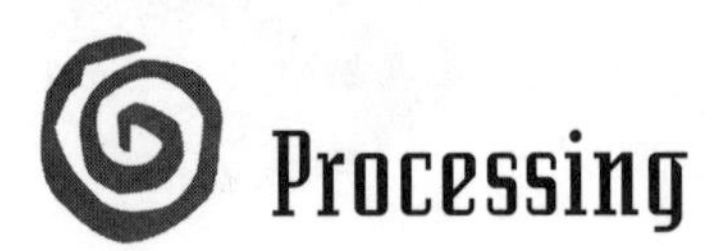

Processing

Christians often say they've been "born again." Although many of us are adults when we put our faith in Christ, salvation is an act of rebirth. Like a child coming into the world for the first time, a new Christian begins life all over again as a new creation.

The sins of the past are wiped clean by Jesus' blood. Unfortunately, many Christians are like Jessica—struggling to let go of the past and embrace their newness in Christ.

Psalm 103:12 says, "As far as the east is from the west, so far has he removed our transgressions from us." How far is the east from the west? We can't imagine that kind of distance, because it never ends. Our sins couldn't be farther from us, so why do we insist on living as though they're still following us around?

God is without sin, and we are sinful. Imagine how dirty we must seem to him! Yet when we accept Christ, we become clean in God's eyes. If our holy God can see us that way, we should be able to see ourselves that way, too. Who we were and what we did no longer matters. We've all been reborn into a new life with God.

SAVING

Are there any past sins you've been holding on to?

Why is salvation referred to as being "born again"?

How does God view our past sins?

A Purpose for the Pain

Why?

The same question had plagued Ron every day since his father's death three months earlier. *Why did you let this happen, Lord?*

There was no explanation for the car accident that had claimed the life of Ron's father. That's why people called it a "tragedy." It was unexpected and, in Ron's mind, meaningless. "The Lord works in mysterious ways," Pastor James had told him at church. *How are you working through this, God?* Ron wondered.

As he watched his mother and sisters suffering through the loss of their father, Ron felt like he was sitting in the middle of a giant question mark. He had always trusted God's wisdom, but how could anything good come out of something so painful?

DOWNLOAD BIBLE BYTE

Jesus loved Martha and her sister and Lazarus. Yet when he heard that Lazarus was sick, he stayed where he was two more days.
John 11:5–6

Processing

Jesus' reaction to the news of Lazarus' illness is confusing. Jesus had already shown he could heal people (John 5:8; John 9:6). If he'd healed complete strangers, why allow a man he loved to suffer and die? Even though Jesus eventually raised Lazarus from the dead, we're still left with the question of why he allowed Lazarus to die in the first place.

Martha and her sister Mary probably wondered the same thing. They didn't openly question Jesus about his absence during Lazarus' illness, but they both said, "Lord, if you had been here, my brother would not have died" (John 11:21, 32). They had faith in Jesus, but they didn't understand his behavior. We often find ourselves in the same position, wondering why God allows pain in our lives. Even if we have faith that he's powerful and wise, his ways are confusing to us.

Jesus told his disciples, "Lazarus is dead, and for your sake I am glad I was not there, so that you may believe" (John 11:14–15). The pain experienced by Lazarus, Martha, and Mary was not meaningless, but necessary for strengthening their faith and the faith of the disciples.

When pain seems illogical, remember that God *does* work in mysterious ways. No matter how confusing life can be, Romans 8:28 promises, "in all things God works for the good of those who love him." There was an important reason behind Jesus' hesitation to go to Lazarus, just as there is an important reason for everything in our lives.

HIGHLIGHT

We don't have to understand God to trust his goodness and wisdom.

SAVING

Has pain ever caused you to question God's purposes?

When has pain eventually led to something good in your life?

Spirit of Confidence

Cheryl shook her head as she flipped through her high school photo album.

"I look scared to death," she said to her mother, laughing softly. Her humor fizzled quickly as she studied her flushed cheeks and downcast eyes in the photo. "Is this how people remember me?"

Her mother looked over her shoulder and smiled. "You didn't just look scared," she said. "You were scared. I never understood why you didn't have more confidence." Cheryl closed the album and placed it on the bookshelf.

"I was a poor student; I wasn't pretty or popular," she explained. "I didn't think I had anything to be confident about."

"And now?" her mother asked.

"Now I have God," she said. "Because of him, the girl in that picture is a new person."

"So you're not scared about going to your high school reunion next week?"

"I'm looking forward to it," Cheryl said. "I wasn't the only timid girl in school. Maybe I can help someone else see how much God gives us to be confident about."

DOWNLOAD BIBLE BYTE

For God did not give us a spirit of timidity, but a spirit of power, of love and of self-discipline.
2 Timothy 1:7

Processing

The apostle Paul knew Timothy wasn't naturally brave, but it was clear the young man loved God and wanted to tell others about Jesus Christ. When Paul asked Timothy to oversee the church in Ephesus, he knew Timothy would need encouragement to be a leader. Paul reminded Timothy that the secret to being confident is found in our relationship with God.

Different people draw confidence from different things. Some depend on physical appearance, others on talent, and some on wealth or social standing. Regardless of what our gifts are, many of us still struggle with confidence. Timothy knew Paul loved him dearly and had confidence that he could perform the tasks set before him, but Timothy was still timid and scared of failure.

We are not wrong to doubt our own strength. Paul did not tell Timothy to have confidence in himself. Instead, Paul told Timothy to remember the qualities of God. When we become God's children, he fills us with his Spirit. We can find confidence in the knowledge that our Father's Spirit resides in our hearts, and his Spirit is powerful, loving, and triumphant over sin.

HIGHLIGHT

Self-confidence comes not from our own qualities, but from the qualities of God's Spirit residing within us.

SAVING

Why wasn't Cheryl confident in high school?

Where do you find your confidence?

How might the attributes of God's Spirit be reflected in the lives of humans?

Rewards for the Righteous

Greg broke into a run when he spotted the police cars parked near his house. "What's going on?" he shouted when his father appeared by the curb. "Are you and Mom okay?"

"We're fine," his dad said, nodding at the house across the street. "It's the Cains. They were robbed."

Greg shook his head as he watched Mrs. Cain tearfully give her statement to an officer. Of all the people on the block, why did the Cains have to suffer? Last year they'd lost a son to cancer and two months ago Mr. Cain had been in a serious car accident.

Greg didn't know what he thought of the Cains' Christian beliefs, but ever since he was a child Greg always had the sense the Cains were living faithfully to their God. When he went to their house to play with Mr. and Mrs. Cain's son, John, he often saw Mrs. Cain reading her Bible. The Cains were also churchgoers.

And what do they have to show for it? Greg thought. *Instead of receiving blessings for their good deeds, they get one heartache after another. I hope one day their God will reward them.*

DOWNLOAD BIBLE BYTE

"I the Lord search the heart and examine the mind, to reward a man according to his conduct, according to what his deeds deserve."
Jeremiah 17:10

Processing

Greg would probably be doubtful if he read the verse above. He's not the only one who has a hard time believing God rewards his faithful followers. Many of us have seen praiseworthy Christians like the Cains run into nothing but hardship. But regardless of how doubtful we might be, the Bible promises a reward for those who please God.

Job's life shows us how God blesses faithfulness. Job suffered physical and emotional pain unlike anything we can imagine. Yet even when his own wife told him to "curse God and die," he remained faithful to his Lord (Job 2:9). When Job persevered through his trials, God was pleased, and Job 42:10 says, "the Lord made him prosperous again and gave him twice as much as he had before."

Not all of us will see God's rewards as Job did. The Bible also speaks about God's children receiving their rewards in heaven (Matthew 5:12), and perhaps that's where the Cains would receive their reward. But no matter where, when, or how God chooses to reward his children, he's promised to reward those who obey and please him. Psalm 62:12 says, "You, O Lord, are loving. Surely you will reward each person according to what he has done."

SAVING

How has God rewarded you or your family?

Why do you think God waits to reward some people?

What is the danger of focusing too much on our reward?

Too Much to Handle?

"One more lap, Henry," Coach Curtis yelled at Washington High School's star sprinter.

Henry shook his head and slowed as he approached the coach.

"I can't, coach. I have to stop." Bending over, Henry fought for air. He'd already sprinted farther than ever before, and his body couldn't handle another lap.

"Don't stop now, Henry. I said one more." The coach pressed a hand against his back, indicating he wouldn't tolerate an argument.

Henry forced his legs into motion, but couldn't push himself past a jog. Henry thought he heard his coach yelling, but the pounding in his ears muffled whatever the man was saying.

Chills ran up and down Henry's arms and his lungs burned as he felt a cloud of numbness sweeping through his body. *It's too much for me*, he thought, turning to look across the track at Coach Curtis. The man continued to shout encouragement until Henry collapsed from heat exhaustion.

DOWNLOAD BIBLE BYTE

"Before I formed you in the womb I knew you, before you were born I set you apart."
Jeremiah 1:5

Processing

Sometimes we don't feel ready to do the things God asks us to do. When God told Jeremiah he would be a prophet, the young man was frightened. The people in Jeremiah's day had turned away from God, so preaching to them was a scary idea. He resisted God's calling saying, "I do not know how to speak; I am only a child" (Jeremiah 1:6).

Jeremiah and Henry shared the same fear—inadequacy. They didn't believe they were able to do what had been asked of them. Henry felt the warning signs in his body. He knew another lap would be too much for him, but his coach disagreed. Unlike Henry's track coach, God knows perfectly well what we're capable of, and he won't give us more than we can handle.

God makes His plans for us based on knowledge, and his plans are perfect because he's known us since before we were born. When fear threatens to disable you, remember the words of Jeremiah 29:11: "'For I know the plans I have for you,' declares the Lord, 'plans to prosper you and not to harm you, plans to give you hope and a future.'" He knows you better than you know yourself, so trust his ways and live life with the courage that comes from faith in his wisdom.

SAVING

When have you felt inadequate?

Why are God's instructions more trustworthy than those of Henry's coach?

How do we know we're able to do what God asks of us?

Why Ask Why?

Karen closed her suitcase and took one last look around the empty bedroom. Even without furniture or decorations, she could remember every one of her sixteen years in the little room.

"Let's go, Karen," her mother called. "The moving van's ready to leave!"

"I'm coming," she yelled back. With a tired sigh she lifted the suitcase, thinking it felt as heavy as her heart.

The news that Karen's family would be leaving had come unexpectedly. Her father's new employer wanted him on the west coast ASAP. Perhaps if there'd been more time to adjust to the idea Karen wouldn't be as troubled, but she'd only had a few weeks to say goodbye to her childhood home.

"Why is this happening, Lord?" she whispered. "What are you going to accomplish by taking me away from the place I love most?"

DOWNLOAD BIBLE BYTE

And we know that in all things God works for the good of those who love him, who have been called according to his purpose.
Romans 8:28

Processing

When going through a hard time, we often have difficulty seeing God's purpose in it all. We get discouraged. Sometimes we even question God's wisdom.

While facing adversity it's important to remember that we only make things worse when we fail to trust God. Yes, it is hard to see what God is up to sometimes, but that is never an excuse to doubt his goodness or power or intelligence. Consider this: If we came from God and yet we suspect that God is mean or incompetent, what does that say about us? How can we be any better than the one who created us?

Job once questioned God, and here is what God said to him: "Where were you when I laid the earth's foundation? Tell me, if you understand. Who marked off its dimensions? Surely you know! Who stretched a measuring line across it? On what were its footings set, or who laid its cornerstone—while the morning stars sang together and all the angels shouted for joy? Who shut up the sea behind doors when it burst forth from the womb, when I made the clouds its garment and wrapped it in thick darkness, when I fixed limits for it and set its doors and bars in place, when I said, 'This far you may come and no farther; here is where your proud waves halt'?" (Job 38:4–11). A God this powerful is certainly worth our trust.

SAVING

When was the last time you had a difficult time trusting God?

Why do you think God leaves the future unknown?

What should our attitude be about the uncertainties of life?

Worthless Worrying

Trudy let the drapes fall across the window and turned on the TV. The weather report predicted snow later in the evening. "If you'll be on the roads, take extra caution tonight," the forecaster warned. Trudy turned and pulled the drapes aside again.

Larry wasn't late, but Trudy was worried anyway. *What if the snow already started in the mountains?* she thought. The road to Larry's was always slippery, even without newly fallen snow. As Trudy stared at the gray sky, her mind filled with tragic scenarios. She pictured Larry's car sliding across the ice and over a cliff.

Five minutes later, Trudy was relieved when Larry's truck pulled into her driveway. He was safe for the moment, at least. *But what about the ride home?* she wondered, a new wave of worry crashing over her.

Processing

Worry is an enemy people fight against on a daily basis. The Bible tells us not to worry, but banishing those nagging fears and doubts from our minds is easier said than done. Life is full of unknowns that we can't control.

Even though worrying seems natural, common sense tells us it doesn't do any good. Luke 12:25 says, "Who of you by worrying can add a single hour to his life?" Worrying doesn't accomplish anything except to

DOWNLOAD BIBLE BYTE

Those who trust in the Lord are like Mount Zion, which cannot be shaken but endures forever. As the mountains surround Jerusalem, so the Lord surrounds his people both now and forevermore.
Psalm 125:1–2

make us more fearful about uncertainties in our lives. Trudy's fear was a dominating influence that consumed her thoughts, but what good came from it?

Worrying is more than a waste of time; it's also sinful. It's like saying to God, "I don't believe you're in control or that you really love me." Why worry if we trust God's power? Why worry if we believe he works everything for our good (Romans 8:28)? Psalm 125 reminds us that God's power and protection are always with us.

Worry is just a weapon Satan uses to pull us away from God. When facing the unknown, resist worry and trust God, who will "fill you with all joy and peace as you trust in him, so that you may overflow with hope" (Romans 15:13).

> **HIGHLIGHT**
>
> "Worry a little bit every day and in a lifetime you will lose a couple of years. If something is wrong, fix it if you can. But train yourself not to worry. Worry never fixes anything."
> —Mary Hemingway, wife of Ernest Hemingway

SAVING

What did Trudy's worry say about her faith in God?

Why is worry a waste of time?

Why is worry sinful?

The Hope of Heaven

"Life seems so hard right now," Jean told Kate. "Everything feels hopeless."

"It won't last forever, Jean," Kate said sympathetically. "There's always hope." The girls fell silent as Jean thought about her friend's words.

"I wish I could feel hope," she told Kate. "But I don't."

"I know," her friend said. "But if nothing else, you have the hope of heaven."

"Yeah," Jean mumbled, but her reply lacked conviction. "Hey, what do you think heaven is like, anyway? I mean, Christians always talk about it, but what is it? How is it supposed to give me hope if I can't even imagine what it's like?"

DOWNLOAD BIBLE BYTE

"No eye has seen, no ear has heard, no mind has conceived what God has prepared for those who love him."

1 Corinthians 2:9

Processing

One day we'll be in heaven. It's a fact every Christian knows but few really appreciate. Few of us think much about the hope of heaven unless we're going through intense suffering. Maybe that's because heaven is beyond our understanding. Sometimes it seems like a distant dream, and it's hard to feel real hope about something we can't imagine. What is heaven like?

Revelation gives us a detailed picture of heaven. John writes, "Now the dwelling of God is with men, and he will live with them. They will be his people, and God himself will be with them and be their God" (Revelation

21:3). In heaven we'll no longer be separated from God as we are now. We'll experience his love at its fullest.

John also writes, "He will wipe every tear from their eyes. There will be no more death or mourning or crying or pain" (Revelation 21:4). Heartache doesn't exist in heaven. No wonder heaven is hard for us to imagine!

Heaven may seem like a dream, but it isn't. It's a reality. In fact, our heavenly home is more real than our earthly home because the one passes away, while the other is as eternal as God himself. When life weighs us down, it helps to remind ourselves of what God has in store for us. Heaven is a hope that can carry us through anything. We just have to remember it's out there.

SAVING

How do you picture heaven in your own mind?

What do you think is the most exciting thing about heaven?

Why do many people struggle with the hope of heaven?

Relationships

Relationships
Relationships

Body Parts

Craig smiled proudly from his pew as the teen missions team finished their report on a recent trip to Mexico. *They really served God down there,* he thought, a twinge of envy striking his heart.

Craig had wanted to go on the trip, but he knew the physical labor and camping would have been impossible with his crippled leg. Instead of traveling with the other teens, Craig had spent months helping to organize, plan, and raise funds for the trip. Now as he listened to the testimony Craig wished he could have been more involved. *I could have done something more important*, he thought.

Moments later Craig was taken by surprise when one of the teens on stage looked directly at him and said, "The work we did in Mexico was very important, but we couldn't have done it without the help of Craig Tanner. Craig, without your service this trip wouldn't have happened. Thank you."

Craig blinked back tears, speechless as the congregation joined in applause of his behind-the-scenes role in the Mexico missions trip.

DOWNLOAD BIBLE BYTE

The body is a unit, though it is made up of many parts; and though all its parts are many, they form one body. So it is with Christ.
1 Corinthians 12:12

Processing

The Bible says Christians are members of one body, united through faith in Jesus Christ. In spite of our unity as the "body of Christ," we're all unique, with different interests, talents, and opportunities. Sometimes we focus too much on our differences, forgetting that every believer plays an essential role in supporting the body of Christ.

Consider a missionary and a church secretary. Some would say the missionary's work overseas is more valuable than that of the church secretary, but according to 1 Corinthians 12:18, "God has arranged the parts in the body, every one of them, just as he wanted them to be."

Because he worked in the background, Craig thought his tasks were secondary to those of the teens who went on the missions trip. According to 1 Corinthians 12:17 and 19 Craig was wrong: "If the whole body were an eye, where would the sense of hearing be? . . . If they were all one part, where would the body be?" The next time you consider how important your role within the church is, remember that the body of Christ is only as strong as its weakest body part.

HIGHLIGHT

"A river is powerful because many drops of water have learned the secret of cooperation."
—Anonymous

SAVING

To which body part do you liken yourself?

How can you use your unique gifts to support the body of Christ?

What determines how important a person's role is within the church?

Anything for a Friend

“Hello?” Jess sang into the phone, smiling when she heard a familiar voice.

“Jess, it’s Amanda. Will you be around tonight?”

“Yeah. Want to come over?” Jess asked, excited at the thought of spending a Wednesday evening with her best friend.

“Actually, I have other plans. But I need some help,” Amanda replied, and Jess recognized the mischievous tone in her voice. “Mark asked me out, but my mom’s on her ‘no dates during the week’ kick. So can you cover for me?”

“Are you asking me to lie?” Jess asked, not sure how to respond.

“If my mom calls, just tell her I ran to the store or something.”

“Amanda, I don’t know . . .”

“Jess, you’re my best friend. I need you. Please do this for me?” The desperation in Amanda’s voice pulled at Jess’s heart.

“Okay,” she sighed. “Just this once.”

DOWNLOAD BIBLE BYTE

You were running a good race. Who cut in on you and kept you from obeying the truth? That kind of persuasion does not come from the one who calls you.
Galatians 5:7–8

Processing

The apostle Paul wrote the words of this Bible Byte to the members of the Galatian church because he knew they were being influenced by false teachers. These teachers taught that Christ’s death on the cross wasn’t enough to save them from their sins, and eternal life had to be earned by following the rituals of the Jewish law. Paul was upset because these beliefs kept the Galatians from completely trusting in Jesus.

The Galatians believed Paul's message when he visited them, but in his absence they were swayed easily by other teachers. The same thing can happen with our friends. We're influenced by the people we spend time with, and that's why it's important to be careful when choosing your friends. Proverbs 13:20 says, "He who walks with the wise grows wise, but a companion of fools suffers harm."

Consider the friendship between Amanda and Jess. Amanda wasn't pushing Jess to drink, steal, or do anything illegal, but that doesn't matter. Lying is harmful and wrong, and if Amanda could convince Jess to do it once, who says it couldn't happen again? Jess ended up compromising her convictions in the name of friendship. But if you use discernment in choosing your companions, your friendships will lead to growth and wisdom.

HIGHLIGHT

"Friendship is almost always the union of a part of one mind with a part of another."
—George Santayana, best-selling novelist

SAVING

How did the false teachers' message keep the Galatians from "obeying the truth"?

Why were the Galatians influenced by the false teachers?

What kind of friend would help you "grow wise"?

Fleeing the Irresistible

t's getting late," Troy whispered against Sarah's neck. She turned her head and kissed him again.

"Stay here tonight," she pleaded. The words hung in the air unanswered as Troy tightened his arms around her. With Sarah's parents out of town, there wasn't anyone to prevent him from spending the night. *No one but her,* he realized. *Or me.*

"I can't," he said softly, but didn't pull away as she held him.

"We don't have to do anything," she whispered. "We'll just sleep. That's all." The offer was tempting. *Too tempting,* Troy realized as his body begged him to stay. Promises he and Sarah had made echoed in Troy's mind. *Pure until marriage*, they'd vowed. Were they strong enough to sleep together without having sex?

"I have to leave," Troy said abruptly, rising from the couch and leaving the room before he could change his mind.

DOWNLOAD BIBLE BYTE

She caught [Joseph] by his cloak and said, "Come to bed with me!" But he left his cloak in her hand and ran out of the house.
Genesis 39:12

Processing

Joseph was a faithful servant of Potiphar, but Potiphar's wife refused to leave Joseph alone to fulfill his duties to her husband. She saw that Joseph was "well-built and handsome" (Genesis 39:6), and she repeatedly asked him to have sex with her. The offer was probably tempting to Joseph. Even if he wasn't attracted to Potiphar's wife, Joseph was a servant, so refusing to obey the woman could lead to death.

Joseph's reaction to Potiphar's wife shows us how we should respond to temptation. Rather than giving in to temptation, Joseph fled from the situation. He knew he'd eventually surrender to the request if he remained with the woman. The only way for Joseph to escape sin was to escape Potiphar's wife.

First Corinthians 10:13 says, "When you are tempted, [God] will also provide a way out so that you can stand up under it." There's always a way out. Sometimes we're strong enough to say no and stick to our words. Other times running from a tempting situation is the only way to resist sin. Troy and Sarah promised to remain pure until marriage, but their words alone weren't strong enough. Troy knew he had to leave if he was going to resist temptation. Don't hesitate to flee from tempting situations. There's no shame in admitting weakness, but there *is* shame in sin.

HIGHLIGHT

"If you're trying not to eat the forbidden fruit, stay away from the forbidden tree."
—Anonymous

SAVING

What is your typical response to temptation?

Why did Joseph run from Potiphar's wife?

Why don't we ever have an excuse for failing to resist temptation?

Controlling the Warrior Within

re you denying that you flirted with her?" Jill asked, fighting angry tears. Nick shook his head solemnly.

"No, I'm just saying it didn't mean anything."

"How can you say that?" Jill's voice rose as she took a step closer to her boyfriend.

"Jill, I'm sorry," Nick said again, but he could see his words weren't helping. Jill's eyes narrowed and flashed with anger.

"I should have known I couldn't trust you," she said, her lip curling in disgust as her gaze traveled over him. "How can I expect you to be faithful when your father's a cheater?" Jill knew how sensitive he was about his father's affair.

"How dare you bring him into this," he said, wishing he could take back his apology.

"You're the one who brought him into this," Jill said. "Because you're just like him!"

DOWNLOAD BIBLE BYTE

Better a patient man than a warrior, a man who controls his temper than one who takes a city.
Proverbs 16:32

Processing

In writing this proverb Solomon went against the grain of a society that placed high value on military power and skill. He said a patient man was more valuable than a warrior. Today most of us do not fight with traditional weapons of war. We engage in battles of the tongue, and when we lose our tempers, we "take a city" by lashing out with words.

Jesus had plenty of reasons to lose his temper, but he never let his emotions get the best of him. Throughout his life people doubted, challenged, and ridiculed him. Jesus could have destroyed anyone he wanted to, but he never let his temper consume him. Jesus' words, even when forceful, were always controlled and full of truth.

When we're angry, it seems like it would be a relief to tell off the person who is responsible for upsetting us. But Jill's angry outburst only sparked further conflict. Proverbs 15:18 says, "A hot-tempered man stirs up dissension, but a patient man calms a quarrel." Rather than allowing feelings of anger to turn our tongues into weapons, we should remember that wielding weapons is usually not a solution. We should control our tempers and with patience calm our quarrels.

SAVING

How could Jill have responded differently to reflect the values of Proverbs 16:32?

When have you "taken a city" with your words?

Why do you think Jesus controlled his tongue?

Accountability in Friendship

"Thanks for helping," Alex said, handing Darren a paintbrush.

"No problem," Darren said. He watched Alex as they slapped green paint on the front porch shutters. "How are things going with Kim?" Darren asked, noticing a muscle twitch in his friend's jaw.

"Okay," Alex said.

"Seems like you two have been spending a lot of time alone together." Darren knew Alex was uncomfortable, but as accountability partners they'd promised to discuss *every* issue, even the tough ones.

"What's your point?" Alex asked, feigning ignorance. Darren put his brush down and faced his friend.

"Are you sleeping with her?" he asked. Alex stopped painting but refused to look at Darren. His shoulders drooped as he stepped away from the shutters.

"No," he mumbled, "But we've come close a couple times."

"Why didn't you tell me?" Darren asked gently.

"Because I know I've messed up, and I was scared of what you'd say."

"I'm your accountability partner, Al," Darren reminded him. "I'm here to help, not criticize."

"I know. And I'm glad you asked about this," Alex said. "It'll help me keep things under control with Kim."

DOWNLOAD BIBLE BYTE

Wounds from a friend can be trusted. . . . As iron sharpens iron, so one man sharpens another.
Proverbs 27:6, 17

Processing

What does it mean to be "accountable" to someone? Alex and Darren called themselves "accountability partners" because they had made a commitment to hold each other responsible for one another's actions. If one of them was tempted to sin, the other reminded him of God's teaching.

Accountability can be stressful to a friendship when its purpose isn't clear to both partners. When friends confront each other's sinful behavior, someone usually gets hurt. But the verses above remind us that not all wounds are bad. Sometimes our pride needs a little piercing so we can turn our sin over to God and walk obediently with him.

God wants our friendships to be challenging, but we must challenge one another with the proper attitude. Darren's questions hurt Alex's pride by forcing him to admit his weaknesses. But the wounds Darren caused could be trusted, because ultimately they strengthened Alex's ability to resist sin. Accountability requires love, honesty, and trust—the ingredients of lasting Christian friendship.

SAVING

What sins might an accountability partner help you resist?

How is accountability to a person different than accountability to God?

What qualities would make a good accountability partner?

Connected through Christ

"Hi. I'm Sam." Kurt looked up from filling soup bowls to accept the hand extended in his direction.

"I'm Kurt," he said. "Nice to meet you. Want to help?"

"That's what I'm here for," Sam said, rolling up his sleeves and grabbing a ladle. "Do you work in the soup kitchen often?"

"I usually come with a group from my church a few times a year," Kurt explained. "I go to Tenth Presbyterian."

"Yeah, I'm here with people from my church, too," Sam said, reaching for a bowl. "Roadside Community."

"Oh," Kurt said, a little too quickly. He knew about Roadside. It was a charismatic church, and most of the stories he'd heard about the church's worship style had made him uncomfortable.

"Something wrong?" Sam asked, frowning. Kurt shook his head and continued pouring soup. He'd always assumed he'd have nothing in common with someone from Roadside. *But we don't seem very different,* Kurt thought, watching Sam out of the corner of his eye. *We're both here because of Jesus. Maybe that's all that matters.*

DOWNLOAD BIBLE BYTE

There is neither Jew nor Greek, slave nor free, male nor female, for you are all one in Christ Jesus.

Galatians 3:28

Processing

In Paul's time this statement would have seemed ludicrous. Racial and religious tensions ran strong between the Jews and Gentiles. Extreme social divisions existed between the wealthy elite and the slaves. Women were viewed as inferior to men and treated as property.

These tensions haven't completely disappeared. The modern world still struggles with racial, social, and gender division, even within the church.

There will always be Baptists and Catholics, rich and poor, men and women. Paul wasn't saying Christianity erased the differences between people. His point was that because of Christ every believer belongs to the same body. We are all equally important to the kingdom of God. In spite of differences in upbringing, personality, and worship style, Christians have something in common on a spiritual level, and they should not look down on each other.

HIGHLIGHT

Christians are like an orchestra. Different instruments play in harmony to create a glorious symphony.

SAVING

Why was Kurt tempted to look down on Sam?

What factors divide you from other believers?

What does it mean to say all Christians are "one in Christ Jesus"?

The Peaceful Umpire

"**Y**ou betrayed my trust!" Jenna yelled into the phone.

"I'm sorry, Jen," Rachel cried. "I wasn't trying to hurt you. I just didn't think!"

"Well, think about it now!" Jenna growled, slamming down the phone.

Night came and went, and the next morning Jenna woke to a knock on her bedroom door.

"Come in," she mumbled.

"Are you going to the football game?" her mother asked.

"Yeah, I guess so," Jenna answered, getting out of bed. When she arrived at the game, she found Rachel sitting alone. It was freezing outside.

"Hi," Rachel said.

"Hello," Jenna replied, keeping her eyes on the field.

The girls sat in stiff silence until the chilling wind grew stronger. Jenna watched Rachel cup her bare hands and blow into them.

"Are you cold?" Jenna asked. Rachel nodded and rubbed her fingers. "Take this," Jenna said, offering one of her mittens. Rachel smiled as she took it.

"Thank you," she said. Jenna nodded and slid closer to block her friend from the wind.

"You're welcome."

DOWNLOAD BIBLE BYTE

Let the peace of Christ rule in your hearts, since as members of one body you were called to peace.
Colossians 3:15

Processing

Peace isn't easy to come by when we've been hurt by somebody. The Bible tells us to love one another, but there are times when we disobey. Sometimes we feel angry, annoyed, or frustrated, and resolving a conflict is the last thing on our minds. But no matter what we feel like doing, our behavior should always promote peace.

In the Greek language, the word for "rule" means "to act as umpire." Peace isn't an emotion; it's a behavior. Being ruled by peace means our actions are determined by whatever will mend a relationship, regardless of our feelings.

Living at peace is especially important among Christians. God wants his followers to be bonded together. Ephesians 4:3 says, "Make every effort to keep the unity of the Spirit through the bond of peace." We are "one body," unified by the Holy Spirit.

Being a peacemaker isn't easy, but we're told to "make every effort" to avoid and repair divisions between us. Don't be ruled by your emotions. Allow the peace of Christ to act as umpire in your heart.

SAVING

How did Jenna obey Colossians 3:15?

When have you allowed peace to rule in spite of your emotions?

If Christians aren't peaceful with one another, what are some possible consequences?

Impaired Vision

Mandy rolled her blue eyes when Jeff slid into the classroom. Beating the late bell by seconds, he did his usual victory dance and sauntered by her desk. Mandy glared at him as he slapped Mr. Laramie on the back. *He's so disrespectful,* she thought. *What a loser.*

Jeff caught her watching him and winked from across the room. Mandy made a disgusted sound in her throat and rolled her eyes again.

Dream on, she told him in her head. Aside from his lack of manners, Jeff wasn't exactly the handsome type. Mandy had to suppress a laugh as she imagined him trying to fit into her group of friends. The poor guy would stick out like a sore thumb with his tasteless clothes and juvenile "skater" lingo.

Mandy looked over her shoulder at him with an amused smirk. *As if someone like me would ever be interested in someone like him.*

DOWNLOAD BIBLE BYTE

"Why do you look at the speck of sawdust in your brother's eye and pay no attention to the plank in your own eye?"
Matthew 7:3

Processing

Nobody's perfect. In the words of Romans 3:23, "All have sinned and fall short of the glory of God." Not too many people, including Christians, would claim to be without sin. Unfortunately, that doesn't keep us from judging each other.

At times it's easier to point the finger at someone else's mistakes than to fix our own. That's what Jesus was talking about when he spoke to his disciples.

Some people are blind to their own sins but all too eager to draw attention to someone else's. Mandy passed judgment on Jeff. She thought of him as a loser because of his behavior but failed to recognize her own sinful pride.

Judgment isn't always an overt accusation. Many of us, like Mandy, make judgments in our minds and never say a word to anyone. But whatever the case, judgment is God's job. First John 5:3 says, "This is love for God: to obey his commands." He has called us to live according to the teachings of his Word, not to focus on how others are failing to do so.

HIGHLIGHT

God made the rules, so let's leave it up to him to judge the rule-breakers.

SAVING

Why is it hypocritical for us to judge others?

What do we have in common with all people?

What should our attitudes be toward people who sin against God?

Measuring Growth by Suffering

Sharon stared at the soccer team roster in disbelief. She'd never expected to make varsity, but her name was right there at the top of the list.

"Are you surprised, Sharon?" Coach Brandt asked from behind her. Sharon turned toward the coach and shook her head in amazement.

"I don't understand," she said. "I spent most of preseason on the sidelines because of my asthma. I didn't think you'd even noticed me."

"Actually, you stood out to me from the very first scrimmage." When the girl looked even more confused, Coach Brandt smiled.

"Sharon, you put every ounce of your energy into this team, whether you were in the middle of the action or shouting encouragement from the bench. You didn't give up on yourself or this team, even though you could have called it quits with the first asthma attack. That shows character." The coach nodded toward the roster.

"In my book, that puts you first on the list."

DOWNLOAD BIBLE BYTE

Not only so, but we also rejoice in our sufferings, because we know that suffering produces perseverance; perseverance, character; and character, hope.

Romans 5:3–4

Processing

It takes effort for us to think of suffering as something we should rejoice about. Our natural response to trials is to complain and agonize about how miserable we are. But when Paul wrote about rejoicing in our sufferings, he was looking at the big picture. He recognized that difficulties in the present can bring about positive changes in the future.

Trials can turn us into stronger, wiser people if we respond to them with endurance. For example, Sharon's asthma kept her on the bench, but she didn't let it keep her out of the game. Instead of giving in to defeat, Sharon fought to be a part of the team. She endured by becoming an encouragement to the other players even when she couldn't be on the field with them.

When life knocks us down, we have two choices. We can give up and lose ourselves in heartache, or we can persevere and recognize that he is at work within us. James 1:4 says, "Perseverance must finish its work so that you may be mature and complete, not lacking anything." Every suffering is a chance to grow.

HIGHLIGHT

"There is nothing the body suffers which the soul may not profit by."
—George Meredith, English writer

SAVING

How do you usually respond to sufferings?

How did Sharon's perseverance build character?

How has God used sufferings to help you grow?

Proper Priorities

“Summer break, here I come,” Steve said to himself, grabbing his bat and glove. He was meeting his friends at the school’s baseball field for what they all thought was the perfect way to start the summer.

He started down the stairs and stopped. Kristen, his older sister, was sitting on the bottom step, crying.

She looked up at him. “Hi,” she said, and sniffled.

“Hi Kristen, what’s up?” he asked.

“Brad just dumped me.”

“Bummer.”

Now what do I do? he thought. *She looks like she could use a friend, but the guys will be starting any time now. I don’t want to miss it.*

DOWNLOAD BIBLE BYTE

“‘Love the Lord your God with all your heart and with all your soul and with all your mind.’ This is the first and greatest commandment. And the second is like it: ‘Love your neighbor as yourself.’”
Matthew 22:37–40

Processing

Jesus told us plainly what our priorities should be. First, our love for God comes before everything else. This priority involves obedience, according to 1 John 5:3: “This is love for God: to obey his commands.” Second, we’re commanded to love other people. So where does that leave *us*? You got it. Last.

The world takes a different approach. Society preaches we should always seek personal fulfillment. We’re told to be “true to ourselves” and “look out for Number One.” This worldly philosophy is in agreement with the selfish tendencies of our sinful nature, so prioritizing according to Jesus’ guidelines isn’t easy.

Even when we know what our priorities should be, we have a hard time sticking to them. That's because the world tells us, "Do what feels good." Like Steve, maybe we don't *feel* like putting other people before ourselves, but priorities aren't about what we feel; they're about what we do. If we're serious about following Christ's priorities, we'll put ourselves last on the list.

SAVING

How do we show our love for God?

If someone were to judge you by your actions, what would they see as your priorities?

Why is it difficult to put ourselves last?

Hate the Sin, Love the Sinner

"Late night?" Eric asked as Shane walked into his kitchen.

"How'd you guess?" Shane's wry smile showed he was aware of his disheveled hair and the dark circles beneath his eyes. Eric cringed inwardly, knowing he wasn't going to like what his best friend was about to say. Shane's smile widened. "I ran into Jess at the party last night," he said. "Let's just say I didn't get much sleep." His meaning was obvious.

"Shane, why do you do this to yourself?" Eric asked, his expression sorrowful rather than condemning.

"I know you don't approve of my worldly ways, buddy," Shane said, "but I'm having fun."

"It's wrong, Shane. And someday there'll be consequences," Eric said. Shane looked into Eric's pleading eyes and saw sincerity. Shane knew his friend condemned his actions, but he also knew Eric loved him like a brother. *Maybe I should start listening to him,* he thought.

DOWNLOAD BIBLE BYTE

Jesus straightened up and asked her, "Woman, where are they? Has no one condemned you?" "No one, sir," she said. "Then neither do I condemn you," Jesus declared. "Go now and leave your life of sin."
John 8:10–11

Processing

When the Pharisees brought the woman before Jesus, they were hoping he would pass judgment on her. The woman had been caught in adultery, and the law said she should be stoned to death. Instead of sentencing her to death, Jesus told the Pharisees, "If any one of you is without sin, let him be the first to throw a stone at her" (John 8:7). Realizing their own sinfulness the Pharisees left the woman alone.

Jesus didn't condemn the woman, but he also didn't pronounce her innocence. She'd sinned, and Jesus wouldn't excuse her adultery. He told her to leave her old ways and live a pure life.

We should follow Jesus' example with our non-Christian friends. We may feel that if we don't condemn sin, we're condoning it. But the Bible says we shouldn't judge others because we're all sinful (Matthew 7:3; Luke 6:37; Romans 14:10). Jesus' example shows our judgment should be on the sin, not the sinner. His attitude toward the woman may have given her the motivation to leave her sin. We can offer the same encouragement to our friends by showing love even as we take a stand against their sin.

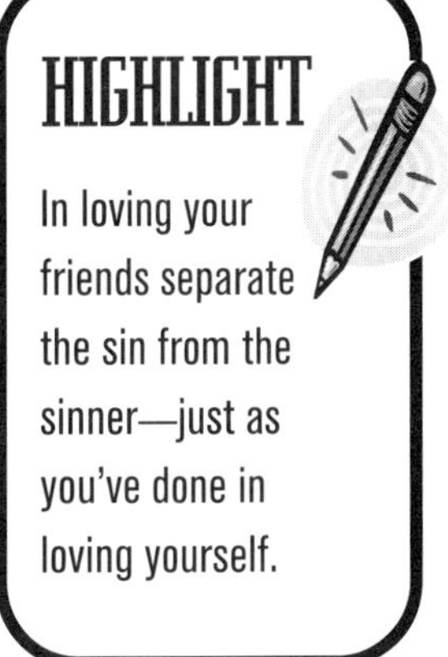

HIGHLIGHT

In loving your friends separate the sin from the sinner—just as you've done in loving yourself.

SAVING

How would you respond to Shane's behavior?

How do you think Jesus' attitude affected the woman?

Why shouldn't we judge people?

Praying for the Persecutor

Shawn stopped in his tracks when he spotted Harold outside the locker room door. Ducking behind a dumpster, Shawn peeked around the corner to see what the older boy was doing. Harold leaned against the school's brick wall, his dark eyes sweeping back and forth over the athletic fields.

He's waiting for me again, Shawn thought miserably. He ran a finger over his upper lip, still swollen from his last encounter with Harold.

Tip-toeing back the way he came, Shawn got out of Harold's sight and breathed a big sigh. Today he'd go the long way home.

"Why is he so mad at you?" his older sister asked when Shawn told her about his escape.

"Because Julia is his ex-girlfriend, that's why."

"I see. You're dating the girl who dumped him, so he assumes you stole her."

"Yeah, and I don't know what to do about it. I mean, I can't keep running away."

DOWNLOAD BIBLE BYTE

"Do good to those who hate you, bless those who curse you, pray for those who mistreat you."
Luke 6:27–28

Processing

Prayer is an act of love. It's easy to pray for people who care about us. The real challenge is in praying for those who are out to hurt us. Jesus had dangerous enemies—people who wanted to see him humiliated, tortured, and killed. Few of us are objects of that kind of hatred, but we still struggle to love and pray for people who are mean to us.

The concern we have for others is evidence that we're sons and daughters of God. Matthew 5:44–45 says to "pray for those who persecute you, that you may be sons of your Father in heaven." God doesn't limit his love to those who love him back. He offers it to anyone willing to receive. If we claim to be his children, our lives should reflect his love.

Romans 5:5 tells us God has "poured out his love into our hearts." It's because of God's love that we're able to show love to others. God's abundant love enabled Jesus to pray for his enemies' forgiveness even as he hung on the cross (Luke 23:34). Just like Jesus, we are sons and daughters of God. With God's love in our hearts, we too can love and pray for those who mistreat us.

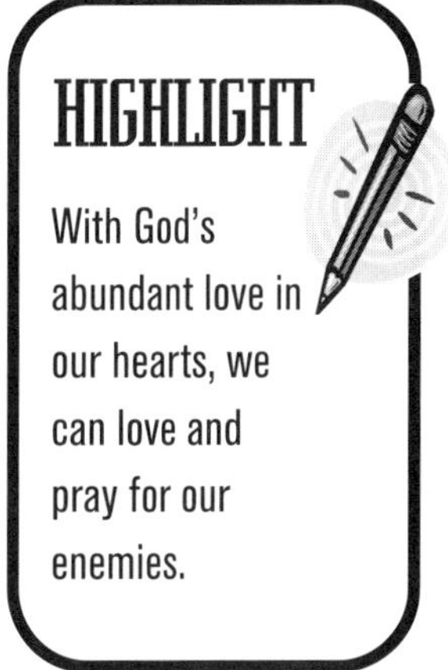

HIGHLIGHT

With God's abundant love in our hearts, we can love and pray for our enemies.

SAVING

How often do you include "enemies" in your prayers?

Whose model should we follow in relating to our enemies?

If you were Shawn's brother or sister, how would you advise him?

A Clean Slate

Heather arrived at church fifteen minutes after the service started. Slipping quietly into the back pew, she glanced around nervously. She hoped no one would notice her presence, but before long a girl several rows ahead turned in her seat, her eyes fixing on Heather. Heather blinked back tears as the girl turned immediately to her friend and whispered something that made several worshipers turn their heads toward the back of the church. Their gazes were cold and unwelcoming, and Heather looked away, clutching the Bible in her lap tightly.

Two months ago Heather had turned her life over to God at a revival service in the local park. At the time, Heather had looked forward to getting to know her new church family, but instead of warm smiles and encouraging words, each week she'd been greeted with indignation and accusatory glances. Heather was aware that she was known for her promiscuity and wild lifestyle, but she'd put those sinful ways behind her. *If God can forgive me, why can't they?* she wondered, slouching in her pew as the congregation rose to sing.

DOWNLOAD BIBLE BYTE

The voice spoke to him a second time, "Do not call anything impure that God has made clean."
Acts 10:15

Processing

God gave the apostle Peter a vision to teach him about the forgiveness of sins. In Peter's day, the Jewish people believed the Gentiles (the non-Jews) could never be considered God's children. Gentiles were seen as dirty and defiled, but Peter's vision taught him that God could cleanse all things.

God's forgiveness doesn't simply strike a line through our list of sins; it crumples up the list and burns it to smithereens. When God forgives us, we're completely transformed by his love. That's why 2 Corinthians 5:17 says, "Therefore, if anyone is in Christ, he is a new creation; the old has gone, the new has come."

Unfortunately, many new Christians find themselves in Heather's situation: judged by other Christians because of past sins. The truth is, none of us are in a position to judge others. Compared to God we're all filthy creatures, blackened by the sins of our hearts and bodies. But God's forgiveness erases our sins so completely that we're clean even in *his* eyes. Considering our own sinfulness and the extent of God's forgiveness, who are we to judge others for their past sins?

HIGHLIGHT

Don't look for old chalk on a new chalkboard. God gives all his children a clean slate.

SAVING

Have you ever been judged for past sins?

Have you ever made judgments about someone based on your knowledge of their past?

Why should we not consider a person's past sins when they have repented before God?

Wise Guys Wanted

Terry took a deep breath on his way to his neighbor's house. "Mr. Sidler?" he said to a man sitting on the front patio. "Do you have a minute?"

"Sure, Terry," the man said, smiling. He motioned toward the other patio chair. "What's on your mind?"

Terry sat down and looked at the ground for a moment. "I need some advice," Terry said, looking up. "My parents are getting a divorce, and I have to decide who to live with," Terry said.

"I see," Mr. Sidler said, and he looked into the distance. The silence made Terry wonder if he had made a mistake in approaching the man. Finally Mr. Sidler folded the newspaper in his lap and settled back into his seat.

"Believe it or not, Terry, I had to make the same decision when I was about your age."

"Really?" Terry struggled to imagine his middle-aged neighbor as a scared teen.

"What did you do?" he asked.

"Sit back and relax; I'll tell you about it."

DOWNLOAD BIBLE BYTE

But Rehoboam rejected the advice the elders gave him and consulted the young men who had grown up with him and were serving him.

1 Kings 12:8

Processing

When we face tough choices, one of the wisest things we can do is ask for advice. Sometimes seeking advice is easier said than done, especially when we want people to think we're independent. But Proverbs 13:10 says, "Pride only breeds quarrels, but wisdom is found in those who take advice."

Advice is only wise if it comes from the right people. When Rehoboam had to decide how to earn the loyalty of the tribes of Israel, he was right to ask for others' opinions. But he made a terrible mistake by listening to the wrong people, and as a result he almost lost his life.

When you need help making decisions, be sure you trust the right people. Proverbs 12:5 says, "The plans of the righteous are just, but the advice of the wicked is deceitful." Turn to a follower of God, someone who can offer wisdom based on knowledge of the Bible. Sometimes our friends can be helpful, but don't write off the possibility of talking to an older person. As Terry discovered, adults were teens once, too. Their experiences might offer some insight into how to make difficult decisions.

SAVING

Whose advice do you usually seek?

What prevents us from asking for advice?

Why is it important to seek the advice of followers of God?

Support System

isa! You're soaked!" Tammy moved back from the door so Lisa could step in from the rain. "I'll take your coat," Tammy said.

"No!" Lisa said, wrapping her arms around herself. Tammy reached out to touch her shoulder.

"I haven't heard from you in months," she said.

"I'm sorry I didn't return your calls," Lisa said quietly, taking a seat on the couch. "I won't be going back to church."

"What's wrong, Lisa?" Tammy asked. Lisa's lips trembled as she stared at the carpet. "You can tell me anything," Tammy said.

"Can I?" Lisa snapped. "Even this?" She stood and let her coat fall open, revealing her swollen abdomen. "I can't face people at church like this."

"Yes, you can," Tammy said. She wrapped her arms around Lisa. "You're not alone. We'll face them together."

DOWNLOAD BIBLE BYTE

And let us consider how we may spur one another on toward love and good deeds. Let us not give up meeting together, as some are in the habit of doing, but let us encourage one another.
Hebrews 10:24–25

Processing

The first-century church suffered severe persecution. Professing faith in Jesus was dangerous for Christians, resulting in imprisonment or death. As the persecution worsened some believers became frightened that their beliefs would be discovered. Some stopped attending the secret church meetings and considered converting to a religion that didn't put them in such danger. In circumstances like these, it's no wonder Paul taught

Christians to be an encouragement to one another! He may have thought that if Christians failed to do so, the church would fall to pieces under the weight of governmental oppression.

Our problems are quite like those of Paul and first-century Christians. We may not like certain decisions our government makes, but we're in no immediate danger of being imprisoned or tortured or executed for our faith in Christ. We do, however, have problems within the church, and so what was true for the Hebrews is still true for us. If we are going to be an active influence for good in the world, we need each other.

The Christians in our churches and youth groups are a gift from God. Take advantage of the bond of faith you share with them, and "spur one another on toward love and good deeds" (Hebrews 10:24).

HIGHLIGHT

Everyone needs a pit crew to help them make it through the race of life.

SAVING

Why did the first-century church's circumstances make it very important for Christians to encourage each other?

What are some of the church's problems today for which Christians need each other?

What can you do within the next few days to be an encouragement to someone in your support system?

Aging Anger

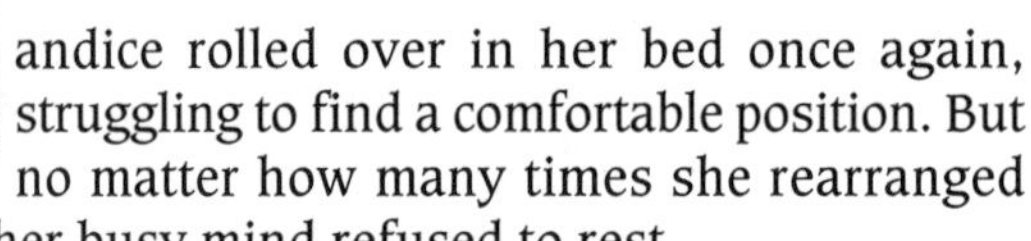

Candice rolled over in her bed once again, struggling to find a comfortable position. But no matter how many times she rearranged herself, her busy mind refused to rest.

Candice mentally replayed the spat she'd had with Mary after church that night. The angry words they'd spoken to one another had been haunting her for hours. *We've just been spending too much time together,* Candice told herself.

She thought about her best friend and all the holiday projects they'd been working on together lately. But instead of remembering Mary's playful sense of humor and enthusiasm, Candice dwelled on her tendency to control everything. *She's always telling me what to do,* she told herself, but as soon as the thought crossed her mind she knew it wasn't true. With a sigh she finally picked up the phone and dialed a familiar number.

"Hello," Mary answered, sounding as restless as Candice.

"Hi," Candice said. "I'm sorry."

"Me too," Mary said softly. "I'm glad you called."

DOWNLOAD BIBLE BYTE

"In your anger do not sin": Do not let the sun go down while you are still angry, and do not give the devil a foothold.
Ephesians 4:26–27

Processing

Aging anger is a dangerous thing. With time, feelings of anger can be transformed into all kinds of sinful thoughts and actions. Bitterness, hatred, and revenge all result from holding on to anger.

When someone intentionally harms us, feelings of anger are natural. The Bible tells us that even God and Jesus have felt anger on occasion. Anger becomes sinful only when we choose to cling to it longer than necessary. The Mosaic law of the Israelites commanded God's people to repay all their debts and wages before nightfall to prevent bad feelings. The wisdom of this old law still applies today. By allowing anger to simmer, even overnight, we give Satan an opportunity to play with our emotions. Given a "foothold," the devil will jump at the chance to feed our anger with bitter thoughts and vengeful desires.

Ephesians 4:31 and 32 tell us to "get rid of all bitterness, rage, and anger," and to be "kind and compassionate to one another, forgiving each other." As soon as Candice recognized her anger was leading to bitter thoughts, she took action to get rid of the negative feelings. Satan can't get a grip on our emotions when anger is followed closely by forgiveness and compassion.

SAVING

How often do you find yourself holding a grudge?

Why is it sinful to hold on to anger?

How can you avoid giving Satan a foothold?

Forever Faithful

When Lindsay first spotted them across the street, she thought she was hallucinating. How could *her* boyfriend be standing there with his arms around a girl she'd never seen? Lindsay's breath caught as Brett kissed the mystery woman.

"This can't be happening," Lindsay whispered. Sharp pain shot through her chest as she watched the embrace. She'd dated Brett for three years, and never had she suspected him of cheating. As she stood paralyzed on the sidewalk, Lindsay's mind raced with thoughts of the future. She'd planned on marrying Brett. They'd talked about getting engaged, discussed where they wanted to live. . . . *We even talked about how many kids we want!*

When Brett finally pulled away from his date, he glanced in Lindsay's direction. She didn't move when their eyes met, and she knew Brett had seen her. His body stiffened for a moment, and he held her icy gaze. Then, as if nothing unusual was happening, he took the hand of the girl beside him and turned away. Lindsay watched their backs until they disappeared around a corner.

DOWNLOAD BIBLE BYTE

For the Lord is good and his love endures forever; his faithfulness continues through all generations.
Psalm 100:5

Processing

Lindsay's experience is painfully familiar to teens as well as married couples. Divorces often result from the same problem Lindsay and Brett faced: unfaithfulness. Unfaithfulness is betrayal, and betrayal makes us afraid to trust anyone.

Some people have a hard time trusting God because of their experiences with betrayal. Many of us have felt the sting of betrayal from friends, boyfriends, or girlfriends, but others have watched their own parents turn their backs on them. If the people who are supposed to love us forever can't remain faithful, how are we supposed to trust God's faithfulness?

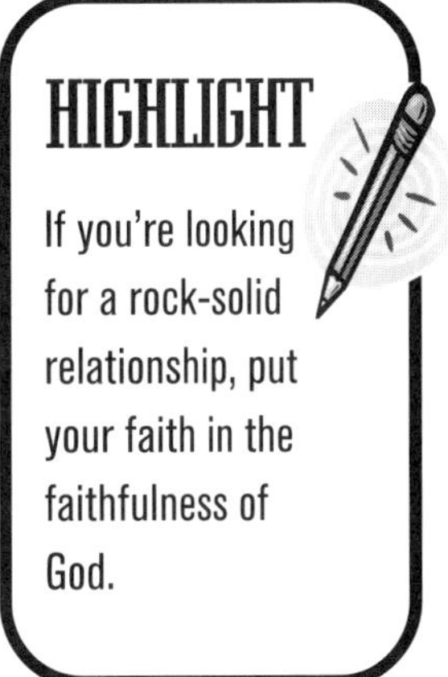

God's faithfulness is nothing like human faithfulness because of who God is. It is impossible for God to break a promise. You might as well wait for birds to fly out of your ears. In Isaiah 54:10 God tells us, "Though the mountains be shaken and the hills be removed, yet my unfailing love for you will not be shaken." His love and faithfulness *will* continue through all generations. Put your trust in him, and he'll never turn his back on you.

SAVING

When have you been betrayed?

How has betrayal affected you?

How is God's faithfulness different from human faithfulness?

More Than Obedience

"My parents are driving me insane!" Lisa vented as she met Alicia in the hallway.

"Now what?" Alicia asked, closing her locker.

"Mom made me wear a coat today. Can you believe that? I know when I need a coat and when I don't. And last night Dad told me to get off the phone. They're a couple of stupid idiots who are completely out of touch with anything that matters."

"Calm down," Alicia said. "I get frustrated with my parents too, but I don't call them names."

"So what? I do what they tell me to do. Who cares what I call them?"

"Well, Lisa, they are your parents."

DOWNLOAD BIBLE BYTE

"Honor your father and your mother, as the Lord your God has commanded you."
Deuteronomy 5:16

Processing

Many people substitute the word "obey" for "honor" in this study's Bible Byte, but obedience is only part of the equation. Honor involves respect and esteem as well. Lisa dishonored her parents by calling them names. She had no respect for them or for their role in her life.

Honoring and obeying our parents is hard, especially when we know how imperfect they are, but God did not say to honor parents when they are perfect. He said to honor them—period. That means putting aside our pride, humbling ourselves, and bringing into our hearts the truth that our parents, though flawed, deserve our respect.

Jesus was perfect. He could have chosen to point out all his parents' flaws, but instead he honored and obeyed them (Luke 2:51), even though he knew better than anyone how flawed they were. We ought to follow Christ's example. Parents may be imperfect, but that's no excuse for failing to honor them. We should also keep in mind that how we treat our parents is a reflection of our relationship with God.

SAVING

What is the difference between honor and obedience?

How have you dishonored your parents?

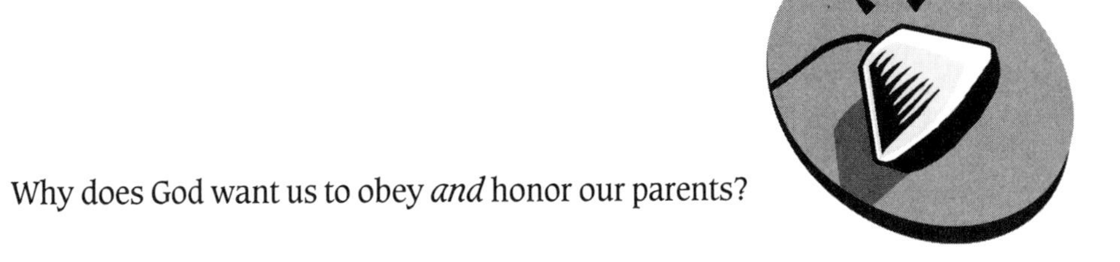

Why does God want us to obey *and* honor our parents?

Picking Fruit

hat on earth were you thinking?" Scott's mother asked him, driving home from the sheriff's office.

"Mom, I wouldn't have done it if it weren't for Tim. I mean, I didn't even have any eggs to start with. Tim had them, and I didn't know about them until he started taking them out of his backpack and giving me some."

"Did he force you to take them?"

"Well, no, but then he starts chucking them at the school and calling me a wimp because I won't join him in the act. Nobody calls me a wimp, so I threw a few too." Scott looked down at his shoes and shifted in his seat. "I guess it was pretty stupid, huh?"

"Yeah, really stupid. You would have been less of a wimp if you'd thrown eggs at Tim! No, no, I'm glad you didn't do that, but I don't want you hanging around Tim any more, okay?"

Download Bible Byte

"By their fruit you will recognize them. Do people pick grapes from thorn-bushes, or figs from thistles? Likewise, every good tree bears good fruit, but a bad tree bears bad fruit. A good tree cannot bear bad fruit, and a bad tree cannot bear good fruit. Thus, by their fruit you will recognize them."
Matthew 7:16–18, 20

Processing

Do we make friends, or do our friends make *us*? For the most part, we have freedom to choose who we want to be friends with. But once we've done that, our friends tend to influence what we become. That's why it's important to choose our friends carefully.

But how do we do that? After all, if we decide to get to know a person *better*, that means we don't really know them in the first place. How do we know who to pursue friendship with?

People show themselves through their "fruit." Matthew 12:34 says, "For out of the overflow of the heart the mouth speaks." A person's words and behavior come from inside to tell us who they are. If we watch closely, we'll see traces of the heart in everything a person does.

If you want a loyal friend, look for someone who works hard at everything they do and never gives up. If you want a helpful friend, watch for someone who's always lending a hand to whoever needs it. Your friends will influence you, so choose people who reflect qualities you'd like to possess in yourself.

SAVING

What are some qualities you look for in friends?

How do you know a person possesses these qualities?

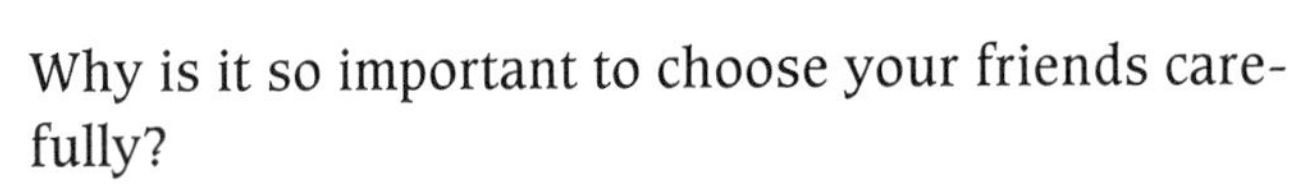

Why is it so important to choose your friends carefully?

Unlimited Forgiveness

"I can't believe you did this!" Rick yelled as he knelt beside a new dent in his car door. "I let you borrow it once and you couldn't even stay out of trouble for one day!"

"I'm sorry, Rick. I swear it was the other guy's fault." Caleb's voice was shaky, and Rick could see his friend was worried.

"Was it the other guy's fault when you totaled my bike last year?" Rick snapped, rising to face Caleb. "Or how about when you borrowed my CDs and they all came back scratched?"

"I'll pay for the damage."

"You bet you will," Rick growled. "And it'll be the last thing you pay for, because I'm never loaning you anything again." He pushed past Caleb, marched into the house, and slammed the door behind him.

DOWNLOAD BIBLE BYTE

Then Peter came to Jesus and asked, "Lord, how many times shall I forgive my brother when he sins against me? Up to seven times?" Jesus answered, "I tell you, not seven times, but seventy-seven times."
Matthew 18:21–22

Processing

Jewish leaders taught that forgiving someone three times was merciful enough, and the fourth offense didn't deserve forgiveness. So Peter thought he was being generous by suggesting seven acts of forgiveness toward the same person. By suggesting seventy-seven acts of forgiveness, Jesus taught that we shouldn't ever withhold forgiveness.

It's easier to follow the "three strikes and you're out" policy than Jesus' principle of unlimited forgiveness. Satan convinces us there has to be an end to second, third, and fourth chances. If someone sins against us over and over again, we have to draw the line somewhere, right?

Wrong. Jesus taught us to pray, "Forgive us our debts, as we also have forgiven our debtors" (Matthew 6:12). When Satan tempts us to put a cap on forgiveness, we should remember where we'd be if God did the same to us. If he only forgave us three, seven, or even seventy-seven times, we'd be doomed. Thankfully there's no end to God's forgiveness. It covers all our sins from birth to death. Because of what he's done, we should extend the same forgiveness to our debtors.

HIGHLIGHT

"Never does the human soul become so strong as when it dares to forgive an injury."
—Croft M. Pentz, pastor

SAVING

Why do we feel a need to limit forgiveness?

Have you ever refused to give someone another chance?

Why should our forgiveness be unlimited?

Background Bigotry

"I'm not proud of my past," Travis said. "Before I became a follower of Christ, my life was full of drugs, sex, and crime." He paused as the eyes focused on him grew large and the room became silent. "But because of God I've given all that up," he continued. "I've made a fresh start. And I came to this Bible study tonight hoping to make some new friends."

When Travis finished his testimony, the teens tried to focus on the night's Scripture passage, but several people seemed more intent on studying Travis than the Bible.

Most of them smiled and nodded when he made eye contact, but one girl in the corner scowled as her eyes traveled over him. He noted the well-worn pages of her Bible and the old date on her "Bible Camp Staff" T-shirt. He shifted uncomfortably and crossed his arms over his brand new Bible, wishing his sleeves covered the tattoos she was staring at with narrowed eyes.

DOWNLOAD BIBLE BYTE

There is neither Jew nor Greek, slave nor free, male nor female, for you are all one in Christ Jesus.
Galatians 3:28

Christians are called to peace and love, but sometimes we struggle with accepting other Christians who come from a different background than we do.

This struggle is nothing new among believers. Like the girl who had difficulty welcoming Travis, Jewish Christians had trouble welcoming Gentiles into the church during the early days of Christianity. The scowling girl likely grew up going to church; the Jews cherished a long religious tradition.

Like Travis whose former ways were anything but pure, the Gentiles came from a nonbelieving background. Yet, both Travis and the Gentiles earnestly desired to follow Christ.

Paul pointed out that we are all on a level playing field, regardless of our background, because we are all sinners. It's true that Travis and the Gentiles were sinners, but it is *equally* true that the scowling girl and the Jews were sinners. Christ and Christ alone is what saves any of us from hell. That's what Paul meant when he said we are all "one in Christ Jesus." With Jesus, the doors of salvation swung wide open to thieves and drug addicts and prostitutes and everybody!

HIGHLIGHT

"After all, there is but one race—humanity."
—George Moore, Irish writer

SAVING

What gets in the way of our Christian calling to peace and love?

How was the scowling girl like the Jews and Travis like the Gentiles?

How are all Christians alike?

From Master to Slave

"Would you girls like some lemonade?" Mrs. Sanders asked, kneeling between Casey and Johanna with a large serving tray.

"Sounds great," Casey said, wiping the sweat from her forehead. She and Johanna had been weeding Mrs. Sanders' garden all morning under the August sun, and they were both ready for a break. As Mrs. Sanders poured the lemonade, Casey noticed the dirt and sweat clinging to their boss's shirt. The woman was working as hard as her helpers even though she was paying them to take care of the garden.

Handing the girls their drinks, Mrs. Sanders stood, saying, "Can I do anything else for either of you?" Casey and Johanna shook their heads and watched Mrs. Sanders walk away.

"She's amazing," Johanna said. "You'd think we were the ones paying her to work!"

"I know," Casey agreed, taking a sip of lemonade. "She sure doesn't act like a boss."

DOWNLOAD BIBLE BYTE

"Now that I, your Lord and Teacher, have washed your feet, you also should wash one another's feet. I have set you an example that you should do as I have done for you."
John 13:14–15

Processing

When Jesus knelt to wash Peter's feet, "No," said Peter, "you shall never wash my feet" (John 13:8). Peter wasn't rebelling against Jesus, but he couldn't understand why his Lord would perform such a humble task. Washing another person's feet wasn't pleasant, but Jesus did it to show his love for the disciples.

Jesus showed that even leaders must be humble and willing to serve. He knew the disciples considered him better than themselves, but rather than acting superior he knelt down and wiped the dirt off their feet with his own clothing. By telling us to wash one another's feet, Jesus asks that we show the same humility and service to others, regardless of their opinions of us.

Servants are usually thought of as inferior human beings, but Jesus has shown us otherwise through his actions and death on the cross. Regardless of what society teaches about servants, Philippians 2:6–7 tells us to imitate Christ "who, being in very nature God, did not consider equality with God something to be grasped, but made himself nothing, taking the very nature of a servant."

SAVING

What does Jesus teach us about leadership?

What good might come from being a servant in your relationships at home and at school?

What can you do in your immediate circumstances that would be comparable to washing another's feet?

The Procrastination Generation

"Dead?" Seth whispered, as his father's news sunk in.

"I'm sorry, son," his father said. He put a hand on Seth's shoulder. "They say the other car was going so fast, it happened instantly. I'm sure he didn't feel a thing."

"Wyatt's dead?" Seth repeated. "I never apologized," he mumbled. "I thought . . ." He swallowed, but the tightness in his throat only worsened. The two sat together for several minutes.

And then, finally, "It's going to be all right, son," the father said. He pulled his son closer. "I'm sure he knew you were sorry."

"No!" Seth said, standing suddenly. He wiped angrily at his damp cheeks and paced the room. "I tried to steal his girlfriend, Dad! How could I have done that and not apologized?"

"Seth, you didn't know . . ."

"I thought I had time," Seth said. "I thought I could wait a little longer, but," he stopped in front of his desk and picked up a framed picture of himself and Wyatt as boys, "I waited too long."

DOWNLOAD BIBLE BYTE

A little sleep, a little slumber, a little folding of the hands to rest—and poverty will come on you like a bandit and scarcity like an armed man.
Proverbs 6:10–11

Processing

Procrastination. It's doubtful there's a person alive who doesn't procrastinate. Even the most organized, disciplined people push aside unpleasant responsibilities. "I'll get around to it," they say, but what happens? As the proverb above warns us, procrastination often results in missed opportunities.

Considering our time-conscious society, it's shocking that procrastination is a problem for so many of us. We want fast food, high speed limits, and express checkouts because we're obsessed with saving time. Yet when it comes to the tedious or unpleasant things in life, we'd rather sit on a couch and stare at the wall than do what needs to be done.

Ephesians 5:15–16 says, "Be very careful, then, how you live—not as unwise but as wise, making the most of every opportunity." Time is a gift, but it won't last forever. None of us knows how long we have to get around to the things we push aside. Seth learned a hard lesson from his procrastination, but we don't have to feel regret as he did. We can learn from Seth's mistake by treating every moment as a gift.

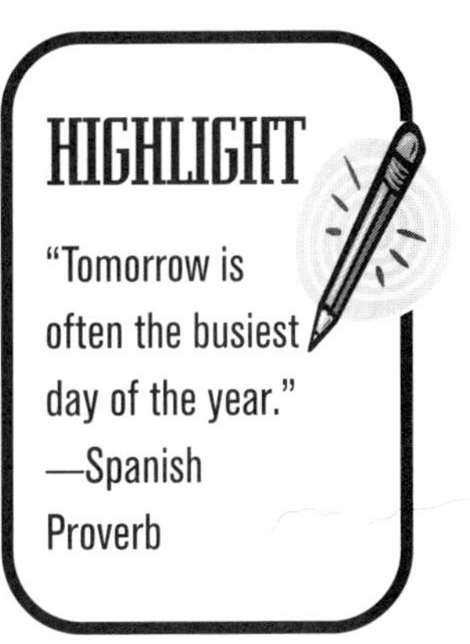

HIGHLIGHT

"Tomorrow is often the busiest day of the year."
—Spanish Proverb

SAVING

Why do we procrastinate things that we know have to be done?

Why is it unwise to procrastinate?

What kind of attitude would make it easier for us to resist procrastination?

God's Plan for Sex and Marriage

"I guess we should say goodnight," Ellen said sadly. She pressed her hands against Chris' chest, but his arms didn't loosen.

"Chris," she said, reading the question in his eyes. "You know I can't let you stay."

"Come on, El. We've waited long enough, don't you think?" he asked. His seductive smile turned to a frown when she wouldn't let him pull her closer. "What's wrong? Don't you want to?" he asked.

"Of course I do," Ellen said. "But that's not the problem."

"I don't get it," Chris groaned. "Why should we wait any longer to have sex? You know I want to marry you."

"But we're *not* married," Ellen argued, stepping away from him. Chris grabbed her hand.

"Please, El," he said, touching her cheek gently. "You know how much I love you."

DOWNLOAD BIBLE BYTE

For this reason a man will leave his father and mother and be united to his wife, and they will become one flesh.
Genesis 2:24

Processing

In the world's opinion waiting to have sex until marriage is an "outdated" practice. These days physical intimacy is considered permissible under just about any circumstances. People indulge in sex as if the union of a man and woman was no different than any other physical pleasure. But God didn't create sex simply as a pleasure for us to enjoy whenever we feel the urge.

God laid out his plan for sex right from the beginning. He created Adam and Eve—one man and one woman. A husband and wife become "one flesh." God created us to be sexually united with one person within the commitment of marriage. Sex outside of marriage is a violation of his plan.

Many unmarried couples struggle with the question, "If we love each other and we're planning to get married, why is sex wrong?" The question can seem complicated, but the answer is simple if we stick to the Bible's teaching. Sex belongs in marriage, and we're not married until we've said, "I do." If two people are committed enough to be planning on marriage, they should also love each other enough to save sex for the wedding night.

SAVING

What do you think is the world's opinion of a Christian commitment to remain sexually pure?

When it comes to physical intimacy, what is the best way for an engaged couple to love each other?

Why do you think God wants us to save sex for marriage?

Rotten with Envy

Helen absently pushed the food around on her plate as Annie's contagious laughter sounded across the cafeteria. "Entertaining her many admirers, as usual," Helen mumbled. She shoved her tray aside and turned to watch the scene behind her.

"Don't you hate people like her?" Stacy asked. "She's perfect."

"Yeah," Helen agreed. "She's always been like that."

"How long have you known her?" Stacy asked.

"Ten years," Helen said. "We grew up next door to each other." Her frown deepened as she reflected on her childhood friendship with Annie. "When we were kids I thought my mom liked her better than me. She was funnier and prettier than any of the other girls. She was always the most popular."

"Not much has changed, I guess," Stacy said.

"Not really," Helen agreed. "Except I hate her even more now than I did then."

Annie laughed again, bringing a round of smiles from her companions. Helen rolled her eyes and looked away, loathing the joyful sound that echoed off the cafeteria walls.

DOWNLOAD BIBLE BYTE

A heart at peace gives life to the body, but envy rots the bones.
Proverbs 14:30

Processing

An envious heart brings about all kinds of trouble. Envy "rots the bones" because it consumes the heart and infects a person's entire being. James 3:16 says, "Where you have envy and selfish ambition, there you find disorder and every evil practice."

Envy is like coveting, which means wanting something that belongs to someone else. God commanded us not to covet (Exodus 20:17) because he knew that envy can divide people, just as it divided Helen and Annie. Envy can lead to quarreling, anger, bitterness, manipulation, stealing, and slander, just to name a few possibilities. If allowed to take root, envy can infect every area of our lives and be the death of our relationships.

First Thessalonians 5:16–18 tells us how we can overcome envy and have peaceful hearts: "Be joyful always; pray continually; give thanks in all circumstances, for this is God's will for you in Christ Jesus." We should thank God for what he's given us instead of focusing on what someone else has. Once we embrace the blessings he's placed in our lives, our hearts can be peaceful, content, and full of life.

HIGHLIGHT

"Our envy of others devours us most of all."
—Alexander Solzhenitsyn, Russian author and historian

SAVING

How did Helen's envy affect her relationship with Annie?

How can we defeat feelings of envy?

How often is your anger toward someone a result of envy?

When We're Weak

While teenagers danced, drank, and laughed inside the house, Patrick sat alone on the front porch. An untouched bottle of beer sat on the railing in front of him, and Patrick stared at it.

"What's up, Patrick?" someone said, coming out the door.

Patrick turned. "Oh. Hey, Cameron," he said.

"I haven't seen you since that church picnic," Cameron said, putting his beer down and eyeing Patrick's full bottle. "You sick?"

"Nah. I shouldn't drink," Patrick said quietly, "but I want to." His jaw tightened. "I used to drink every weekend until I couldn't sit up straight." When Cameron didn't respond, Patrick looked at him again. "Surprised?"

"Yeah," Cameron admitted. "I thought I was the only one." He took a seat next to Patrick. "I mean, I know I shouldn't be doing this, but it's like I can't help it."

Patrick nodded. "It's tough, but I feel better just having told you. It's like a big weight just fell off me."

"Maybe you can help me," Cameron said. "We could help each other."

DOWNLOAD BIBLE BYTE

Therefore confess your sins to each other and pray for each other so that you may be healed.
James 5:16

Processing

Different people struggle with different sins. Patrick and Cameron felt weak when faced with the temptation of alcohol, while others struggle with things like lying, sex, or drugs. But whatever our weaknesses may be, we don't have to deal with them on our own.

God intended for his people to help one another, and confession and prayer are two ways we can do that. By confessing our sins to one another, we become united with others in battling our weaknesses. The prayers and encouragement of another Christian can empower us to conquer guilt, resist further temptation, and obey God in the future.

Unfortunately, many Christians keep their weaknesses a secret. We fear that people will condemn us for the things we've done and the things we struggle with. But when we hide our sins and weaknesses, they fester and grow. When we take the risk of confessing our weaknesses, we often discover a friend with a similar weakness who is willing to help us.

If someone confesses a weakness to you, remember 1 Thessalonians 5:11: "Therefore encourage one another and build each other up." There's no room for condemnation in the body of Christ, but there's always room for prayer.

HIGHLIGHT

Pretending you don't have weaknesses will only ensure that you keep them.

SAVING

What weaknesses do you struggle with?

Why is it unwise to keep your weaknesses a secret?

How does openness about our weaknesses help us overcome them?

A Friend to the Friendless

Julie had been watching the girl in the corner since the youth group meeting began. While everyone sang and clapped to the music, the girl sat on the floor, hugging her knees to her chest as if trying to make herself as small as possible. Her thin black hair fell limply over her timid dark eyes, which shyly drank in the scene before her. When the meeting ended, the girl stood and tugged self-consciously at her T-shirt. She seemed ready to run and hide when she spotted Julie heading her way.

"Hi!" Julie said, smiling brightly and offering her hand. "I'm Julie." At first the girl simply stared at Julie's outstretched fingers. Then, cautiously, she accepted them.

"I'm Marge," she said, her voice barely above a whisper. Her eyes darted around the noisy room, and Julie could see she was uncomfortable in the lively social setting.

"I was going to get a snack," Julie said, motioning toward the kitchen door. "Want to come with me?" The girl's eyes registered surprise at the invitation, but she nodded her head. Julie smiled again, and this time Marge smiled back.

DOWNLOAD BIBLE BYTE

Live in harmony with one another. Do not be proud, but be willing to associate with people of low position. Do not be conceited.
Romans 12:16

Processing

Often people judge us by who we hang around with. That's why there are unspoken rules about eating lunch with special-education students and befriending computer geeks. Regardless of age, most people want to be associated with the popular crowd.

If we did the same in ancient times, we might have never known Jesus. "He had no beauty or majesty to attract us to him, nothing in his appearance that we should desire him" said the prophet Isaiah. As a carpenter's kid, Jesus was certainly not wealthy.

Like Jesus, the poor or unattractive people around us are worthy of our attention. Unfortunately, many of them are hurting from the conceit that keeps people from befriending them. We have something to *give* and *gain* by interacting with "people of low position." Like Julie, we can show the love of Jesus by offering a gift of friendship without thinking of ourselves. And in giving we also *receive*, benefiting from the unique insight, perspective, and knowledge every individual possesses.

> **HIGHLIGHT**
>
> Love as God loves: offering himself to everyone, not just the rich, smart, and beautiful.

SAVING

What factors affect your choice of friends?

Who are the people of "low position" around you?

How can you reach out to those people?

Two Are Better Than One

"Jesse! Table 6 is up," the cook shouted. Jesse waved in the cook's direction and grabbed a tray. The restaurant was packed, and he couldn't remember who'd been seated first or who was still waiting for food.

"Table 6?" he mumbled to himself, flipping open his order pad. "Great," he groaned, seeing the group had been waiting for thirty minutes.

"Jesse, you've got another table," Ned said as he walked by. Seeing Jesse's face, Ned paused. "Hey, you need some help?"

"Nah, I'm fine," Jesse mumbled. But as he hastily stacked plates onto his tray, Ned moved to help him.

"It's a crazy night," he said when Jesse looked at him. "You're not superman, you know."

"Thanks," Jesse finally said. "I guess I could use some help."

DOWNLOAD BIBLE BYTE

When his father-in-law saw all that Moses was doing for the people, he said, "What is this you are doing for the people? . . . You and these people who come to you will only wear yourselves out. The work is too heavy for you; you cannot handle it alone."
Exodus 18:14, 18

Processing

Ever since he'd led them out of Egypt, the Israelites had depended on Moses to be their leader. Moses accepted the responsibility willingly, but he could see the wisdom in his father-in-law's words. If Moses continued to act alone as the judge of the people, he was going to burn out, so Moses called on officials to help him in his duties to the Israelites.

We can't handle everything on our own. Like Moses and Jesse, many of us try to juggle too many responsibilities at once without asking for help. Sometimes we're prideful and don't want to admit we need assistance, or sometimes we don't want to burden other people with our duties. Whatever the excuse, the Bible makes it clear that God wants us to work together. Ecclesiastes 4:9 says, "Two are better than one, because they have a good return for their work."

Don't try to make it through life without depending on other people. God saw from the beginning that humans need one another. He created Eve to be a helper and companion for Adam (Genesis 2:18–24). If you feel like you're in over your head, don't wear yourself out by pressing on without assistance. Reach out to a friend. There's nothing shameful in admitting you need a helping hand.

> **HIGHLIGHT**
>
> "No matter what accomplishments you make, somebody helps you."
> —Althea Gibson Darben, American tennis player

SAVING

In what ways are you like Jesse?

What are some things that prevent you from asking for help?

How do we know God meant for us to depend on others?

Unequally Yoked

e'll wait here for you," Jake told Diane and Beth. He and Ben sat down on a bench as the girls entered another clothing store in the mall.

"How long has your sister been hanging out with Beth?" Ben asked.

"A couple months," Jake said. "Diane invites her over a lot. They've gotten pretty close."

"I'll bet you don't mind that," Ben said, smiling. "She's cute."

Jake laughed and shook his head. "Believe me, I've noticed. She's also funny, sweet, smart. . . ."

"If you feel that way, why is your sister the one inviting her over all the time?"

"I can't date her, Ben," Jake said, shaking his head again. "She's not a Christian."

"But you really like her," Ben said. "Maybe you should give it a try."

"No," Jake said firmly. "I watched my parents' marriage fall apart because my dad isn't a Christian. I'm not going to repeat their mistakes."

DOWNLOAD BIBLE BYTE

Do not be yoked together with unbelievers. For what do righteousness and wickedness have in common? Or what fellowship can light have with darkness?
2 Corinthians 6:14

Processing

A yoke harnesses two animals together for the purpose of pulling plows or wagons. Animals that are yoked work toward the same goals, so they move together and share their workload. The Corinthians were surrounded by people who worshiped false gods, and Paul used the yoke image to warn them about marrying idol worshipers.

Paul's words also apply to dating relationships. When two people don't share a common faith in God, their goals are different. An unbeliever may not want the same things you want, so living for God is harder because there's resistance from your partner. You pull in opposite directions until one partner follows the other.

It's hard to see the harm in dating people with different beliefs, especially when we meet non-Christians who are more loving than some Christians. But if a person isn't committed to God, they're not going to be interested in following Christ. If we're yoked together with other Christians, we'll have the common goal of pleasing God. Rather than struggling against one another, we can work together with our partner as one being, just as God intended (Genesis 3:24).

HIGHLIGHT

"Love does not consist in gazing at each other, but in looking together in the same direction."
—Antoine de Saint-Exupéry, French author and journalist

SAVING

What problems might arise from being unequally yoked?

What are the dangers of dating or marrying a non-Christian?

What are the benefits of dating someone who shares your beliefs?

Emptying the Recycle Bin

"You're late." Dana's voice was quiet but harsh as she glared at Matt through the screen door.

"I know. I'm sorry, Dana. I got stuck. . . ."

"I don't want to hear it," she snapped, turning abruptly and walking into the kitchen. Matt pulled open the door and followed her through the house, surprised by her anger.

"Hey, are you okay? You seem pretty on edge," he said, but she didn't respond. Matt watched as she stiffly yanked open the refrigerator. "Dana, we're going to be even later if you plan on eating before we leave."

"I'm not going anywhere tonight, Matt," she replied evenly, pulling out a soda.

"Look, I said I was sorry. I got stuck in traffic."

"Is that what happened last time?" she asked, turning to face him. "When you forgot to show up at all?"

"Dana, that was months ago!" Matt exclaimed in exasperation. "When are you ever going to forgive me?"

"Oh, I've forgiven you," she said quietly, then shook her head. "But that doesn't mean I'm over it."

DOWNLOAD BIBLE BYTE

Bear with each other and forgive whatever grievances you may have against one another. Forgive as the Lord forgave you.
Colossians 3:13

Processing

What does it mean to forgive others as the Lord forgave us? Well, Jesus was beaten, ridiculed, and hung on a cross to die even though he hadn't done anything wrong. If there was ever a time for Jesus to be angry, bitter, or hateful, it was during those last moments before his death. But when Jesus prayed that day, he didn't ask for revenge. He said, "Father, forgive them, for they do not know what they are doing" (Luke 23:34).

Jesus not only forgave the worst things anyone could do to him, but he also did so without waiting for an apology. That means we're called to offer forgiveness that's *unlimited* and *immediate*. And that's not the end of the story.

When someone wrongs us, we usually either accept their apology or, given time, "get over" our feelings of anger. But consider Dana and Matt. Have you ever noticed how often the hurts we've "forgiven" come back to haunt our relationships? Real forgiveness is *irreversible*. God doesn't say, "I forgive you," and then throw our past sins in our face the next time we screw up. First Corinthians 13:4 tells us love keeps no record of wrongs. Forgiveness isn't something we can take back. It's either permanent, or it isn't forgiveness at all.

HIGHLIGHT

"What riches of grace does free forgiveness exhibit! To forgive at all, to forgive fully, to forgive freely, to forgive for ever!" —Charles Spurgeon

SAVING

What are three characteristics of real forgiveness?

How was Dana's forgiveness different than the Lord's?

Unfading Beauty

Derek quickened his steps as Kris's house came into view. *Can't be late for our first date*, he thought, and smiled. In a way it felt like he was five years too late.

Kris had been his closest friend since sixth grade, yet it had taken him until last week to ask her out. *I was blind,* he thought. Even though he loved everything about Kris now, for years Derek's eyes hadn't seen the beauty right in front of him.

Kris possessed a quiet beauty. Maybe she didn't have the flowing hair, curvy figure, or fashion sense of the girls he'd always been attracted to, but there was a light inside Kris.

Derek smiled as he thought of her joyful laughter and sparkling eyes. She always seemed to be bubbling over with joy, and he couldn't wait to be the one to share it with her.

DOWNLOAD BIBLE BYTE

Your beauty should not come from outward adornment, such as braided hair and the wearing of gold jewelry and fine clothes. Instead, it should be that of your inner self, the unfading beauty of a gentle and quiet spirit, which is of great worth in God's sight.

1 Peter 3:3–4

Processing

When the apostle Paul wrote these words, braided hair, fine jewelry, and fancy clothing were the typical attire of prostitutes. Paul taught that Christian women should avoid these things not only for the sake of modesty, but because their beauty should come from the inside.

We each possess a body and a spirit. While our bodies will eventually weaken and die, our spirits will live through eternity. That's why Paul talked about "unfading beauty." Inner beauty and physical beauty work in opposite directions—one grows through time, and the other fades away. Proverbs 31:30 says, "Charm is deceptive, and beauty is fleeting; but a woman who fears the Lord is to be praised."

Focusing on inner beauty can be a difficult task in a world where so much attention is given to looks. People will most often judge us by the world's standards, but the world's standards mean nothing to our Creator. First Samuel 16:7 says, "The Lord does not look at the things man looks at. Man looks at the outward appearance, but the Lord looks at the heart." Next time you look in the mirror, try to see yourself through God's eyes.

HIGHLIGHT

"It is amazing how complete is the delusion that beauty is goodness."
—Leo Tolstoy, Russian novelist

SAVING

Which type of beauty, inner or physical, do you think people notice about you?

What would God say makes you beautiful?

Who in your life has the most inner beauty?

Family Ties

Bill looked away as he passed Lenny in the hallway before church. "Hi Bill," Lenny said, but Bill didn't respond. He was still angry about the night before. Lenny and Bill were always arguing about controversial issues. Last night Lenny had debated with Bill in front of the youth group, and in the end Bill had been embarrassed by his lack of Bible knowledge.

How long are you going to keep this up? Bill asked himself. His pride was still hurting, and Lenny didn't seem to feel guilty about it. *I'll keep it up as long as it takes,* he decided, determined to get an apology.

But Bill knew Lenny. There wasn't much chance the older boy would offer an apology, especially when he hadn't done anything but hurt Bill's pride. Unless Lenny had a change of heart, the boys could go a long time without speaking. *I don't care*, Bill told himself. *It's not like I have to see him every day.*

DOWNLOAD BIBLE BYTE

Be devoted to one another in brotherly love. Honor one another above yourselves.
Romans 12:10

Processing

Families are supposed to stick together. Brothers fight with sisters, and children fight with parents, but in the end families are bonded by blood and love. In an ideal family no fight is big enough to destroy a relationship. Love and devotion always triumph over conflicts between family members.

When the apostle Paul uses the expression "brotherly love," he means Christians are members of the same family. We're not necessarily blood relatives, but our shared faith in Christ makes us members of the family of God.

Unfortunately, Christians don't always see themselves as family members, so conflicts with our Christian siblings can end up destroying relationships. Unlike our blood relationships, relationships with other Christians seem expendable. If we don't believe we have a lifelong family connection with someone, it's easier to hang on to feelings of resentment and pride.

Knowing how divisive conflicts can be, Paul tells us to "honor one another above ourselves." Honoring someone means showing him or her respect and appreciation, and in order to do that we have to put aside our own anger and pride. Brotherly love is about being devoted enough to our Christian family members that we honor their needs and feelings above our own. With that kind of family connection, no conflict will ever be big enough to divide us.

HIGHLIGHT

Every Christian is your blood relative—we're related through the blood of Christ.

SAVING

What does brotherly love mean to you?

How are you devoted to other Christians in brotherly love?

Why do Christians call themselves brothers and sisters?

Lightening the Load

Calista tightened her arm around Samantha's shaking shoulders as her friend wept. Samantha's sobs tore at Calista's heart, and soon tears were streaming down both their faces.

"I'm so sorry," was all Calista could say. Every time Samantha talked about her parents' divorce, Calista wanted to confront Mr. and Mrs. Everett.

"Don't you have any idea how much your daughter is hurting?" she wanted to ask. But Calista knew the Everetts' divorce was out of her hands.

Frustrated at her helplessness she hugged Samantha a little harder. Samantha returned the hug.

"Thank you, Cal," she whispered. "I don't know what I'd do without you."

DOWNLOAD BIBLE BYTE

Carry each other's burdens, and in this way you will fulfill the law of Christ.
Galatians 6:2

Processing

When Paul talked about the "law of Christ," he was referring to Jesus' teaching that his followers should love one another. In John 13:34 Jesus said, "Love one another. As I have loved you, so you must love one another." How did Christ love? He touched people with leprosy—people whom the Jews labeled unclean and refused to be near, let alone touch. He wept with Martha and Mary when he found out their brother Lazarus had died. He broke social custom to converse with a Samaritan woman. In short, Jesus wasn't afraid to get down and dirty with the gritty stuff of humanity. He was God, yet he lived in the midst of all our pain and sorrow.

As Christians, we're supposed to take on others' burdens with the compassion of Christ. When we "carry a burden" for someone, it's important to remember we're not responsible for fixing him or her. Sometimes we're limited in how involved we can be. Calista couldn't do anything about the divorce of Samantha's parents, but she could sit with Samantha and share the pain her friend was feeling.

Romans 12:15 says, "Rejoice with those who rejoice; mourn with those who mourn." Offering a listening ear or a sympathetic shoulder to cry on is sometimes all we can do to carry another's burdens. Calista may have been frustrated that she couldn't take away Samantha's burden, but her care and companionship had lightened Samantha's load. That's what carrying another's burdens is all about.

HIGHLIGHT

Carrying burdens might not fix the problem, but it *will* lighten the load.

SAVING

How does Christ's example inspire you to love others?

What are some ways you've carried another's burdens?

How was Calista a servant to Samantha?

Wounded by Words

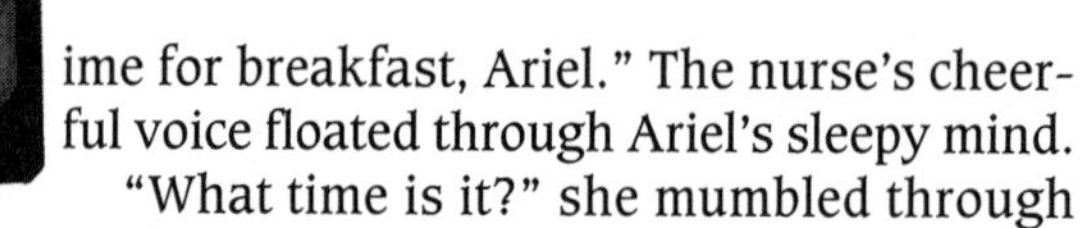

"Time for breakfast, Ariel." The nurse's cheerful voice floated through Ariel's sleepy mind.

"What time is it?" she mumbled through a yawn, opening her tired eyes.

"I told you, honey. Time for breakfast." Ariel returned the nurse's smile and leaned forward as the woman tucked a pillow behind her. "Breakfast" turned out to be a thick liquid drink packed with protein and nutrients. Ariel had been drinking it every morning since checking into the eating disorder clinic to deal with her anorexia.

"I'm so sick of this," she moaned, wrinkling her nose at the artificial cocoa flavor.

"I know," the nurse said. "But keep drinking that and you'll feel different in no time."

Ariel nodded, but inside she asked, *how will I feel different?* After months of starving herself, the clinic's food was helping Ariel's body, but she could still hear the voice of her abusive father, a voice that had pushed her into anorexia.

"You're too fat, Ariel." "You're never going to get a boyfriend looking like that." "You need to lose weight."

Sighing, Ariel took another sip of her breakfast. *Will I ever heal on the inside?*

DOWNLOAD BIBLE BYTE

Consider what a great forest is set on fire by a small spark. The tongue also is a fire, a world of evil among the parts of the body.
James 3:5–6

Processing

There isn't much truth to the saying "Sticks and stones may break my bones, but words will never hurt me." Lashes from the tongue cut deep, often leaving scars in places sticks and stones can't even touch.

Technically, tongues aren't a very powerful body part. They're just little pieces of flesh that help us taste, swallow, and speak. The power of our tongues is in the words they form. The "fire" James mentioned burns inside our hearts and minds. The tongue is harsh when our thoughts are harsh.

Like Ariel, we all know how damaging insults are. Hopefully we also know the healing affect of kind words. Tongues can be a world of evil or an instrument of love, depending on how we use them. James compares the tongue to the rudders of large ships (James 3:4). They're tiny parts in comparison to the whole vessel, but ultimately responsible for the ship's course. We can speak unkind words and take the path of cruelty, or speak gently and follow a course that pleases God.

HIGHLIGHT

"Injuries may be forgiven, but not forgotten."
—Aesop, ancient Greek writer of fables

SAVING

How have words injured you?

When and why have you spoken unkindly to others?

Why do you think unkind words so painful?

Playing Favorites

Jason could tell the congregation was focused on Mayor Prescott as an usher showed him to the front pew of the church. People shifted in their seats and craned their necks to catch a glimpse of the important guest. Even Jason's mother, who never cared much for politics, leaned over the railing to watch the scene below.

The mayor took his seat, and the usher walked back to the entrance, where Jason spotted another newcomer. A gray-haired woman wrapped in a frayed brown cloak and torn stockings crept through the doors and whispered something to the usher. The man frowned and took a few steps back as the woman walked in.

"Humph!" Jason's mother vented. "What's *she* doing here?" she whispered angrily. "Of all days for a homeless woman to drop in, why'd she have to pick the day of the mayor's visit?" Jason didn't respond as he watched people turn to stare at the woman. The usher below dismissed her to an empty pew in the back corner of the sanctuary. Jason saw him roll his eyes at the other usher.

DOWNLOAD BIBLE BYTE

My brothers, as believers in our glorious Lord Jesus Christ, don't show favoritism.
James 2:1

Processing

The members of Jason's church weren't the first to show favoritism. Societies have always drawn lines between people. We make distinctions based on wealth, intelligence, race, and religion, among other things. In Jason's church, the mayor was favored because the congregation valued wealth, power, and fame. The Christians to whom James wrote also showed favoritism to the rich classes.

Why is favoritism forbidden? The answer is simple: "God does not show favoritism" (Romans 2:11). God sent his son to die for the sins of the whole world, not just the handful of rich, famous, and beautiful people at the top of society (John 3:16). If God doesn't show favoritism, then neither should his followers.

It's hard to resist showing favoritism when the ways of the world teach us that some people deserve love more than others. But the Bible tells us our love for others should be unconditional, second only to our love for God (Matthew 22:37–40). We can avoid showing favoritism by not forgetting Christ's universal sacrifice.

SAVING

How does favoritism affect your life?

What does Jesus' life and death tell us about favoritism?

Why do you think favoritism is so common in our society?

What Does God Think of Sex?

Erica took a blank sheet of paper as the youth group leader gave instructions.

"Write a question, fold the paper, and put it in that box," he said, pointing toward the corner of the room. "You're not writing your names, so feel free to ask anything you want."

Erica stared at the paper but wrote nothing. She could already feel color creeping up her neck as she thought about her question. If she couldn't control her embarrassment now, how could she ever hide it when the papers were read aloud?

Glancing around the silent room, Erica wished she could see what others were writing. Would anyone ask about sex? She wanted to know what God thought about sexual pleasure, but it seemed like a forbidden topic. *Why isn't anyone willing to talk about it?* she wondered.

DOWNLOAD BIBLE BYTE

So God created man in his own image, in the image of God he created him; male and female he created them. God blessed them and said to them, "Be fruitful and increase in number; fill the earth and subdue it."

Genesis 1:27–28

Processing

What does God have to say about sex? Oftentimes the church's silence about sex leads to the misconception that God is against sexual pleasure. He must approve of sex for reproduction because he ordered us to "fill the earth." But what about sex for pleasure's sake? Did God intend for sex to be a pleasurable experience?

The Bible answers with a definite yes. Proverbs 5:18 and 19 say, "May you rejoice in the wife of your youth. . . . May her breasts satisfy you always, may you ever be captivated by her love." Song of Songs is an entire book of the Old Testament celebrating love and sexuality as a normal part of married life. God meant for sex to be an expression of love, not just a way to make babies.

The Bible also contains warnings about engaging in sex in inappropriate relationships. Promiscuity, homosexuality, and adultery are forbidden because they violate God's plan for sex between husbands and wives (Deuteronomy 22:21; Romans 1:27; Exodus 20:14). Genesis 2:24 says, "A man will leave his father and mother and be united to his wife, and they will become one flesh." Sex is a gift from God, but it must be experienced as he intended: within the commitment of marriage.

HIGHLIGHT

Sex is pleasurable because God made it that way. He wants us to enjoy his gift when the time and circumstances are right.

SAVING

Why do you think sex is a forbidden topic?

How does your youth group or church experience compare with Erica's?

What restrictions does God put on sex?

More Than Words

Beth wiped her damp cheeks with a tissue and sighed deeply as she opened her bedroom door. Down in the kitchen, she could hear dishes clattering in the sink. Tossing her tissue in the trash can, Beth walked down the stairs.

"Hi, Dad," she said quietly. Her father turned from the sink and smiled softly.

"Hi, sweetheart," he said. "How are you feeling?" Beth shrugged and pulled herself onto a barstool.

"I miss Josh, Dad," she said. "Even though he cheated on me, I still miss him." Her father wiped his hands on a towel and sat down beside her.

"I'm sorry, Beth," he said. "I know you miss him, but you deserve a better relationship than that."

"He said he loved me," Beth said.

"He said that," her father replied. "But he didn't act on his words."

Beth nodded and looked around at the clean kitchen. "You're right," she admitted. "Every Thursday you clean the house so Mom can have a night off. Josh would never have done that for me, even though he said he loved me."

DOWNLOAD BIBLE BYTE

Dear children, let us not love with words or tongue but with actions and in truth.
1 John 3:18

Processing

The message here is not that words of love are meaningless, but rather that they should be accompanied by action. The apostle John, who wrote this verse, knew what he was talking about. After all, he'd spent lots of time around the expert on love—Jesus Christ.

Jesus was a man of action. In John 15:13, Jesus says, "Greater love has no one than this, that he lay down his life for his friends." The greatest love is shown through action, as Jesus proved to us in his own life. The Bible doesn't say Jesus went around telling his followers how much he loved them. Rather, through Scripture we *see* that Christ loved people. Jesus washed his disciples' feet (John 13:5), healed the sick, and fed the hungry (Matthew 14:13–21).

Love is not only active; it's also sacrificial. Jesus gave his life for us by dying on the cross, the ultimate act of love. Beth's father gave his wife a night off, and by doing so sacrificed his own rest and comfort. In the same way, we should prove our love for others by what we do and what we give, rather than by what we say.

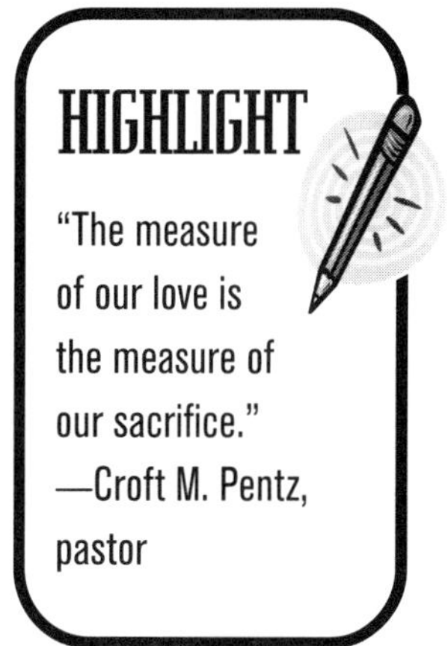

HIGHLIGHT

"The measure of our love is the measure of our sacrifice."
—Croft M. Pentz, pastor

SAVING

How can you say "I love you" without using words?

How do your friends and family express their love for you?

Why is Jesus the ultimate example of love?

Spreading the Word

Spreading the Word

Spreading the Word

Crossing the Line

Stan watched his friends pile into the school van as his class prepared to leave for the field trip. His first inclination was to follow them, but he'd noticed Mark Finley sitting alone in his beat-up Escort. As usual, Mark was driving separately, probably assuming no one wanted to ride with him. Everyone thought Mark was an angry, unfriendly guy. Most people tried to stay out of his way.

Stan heard his friends yelling from the van, but instead of following them, he stepped over to Mark's passenger door.

"Got room for me?" he asked. Mark's face registered shock at the request, but he quickly recaptured his cool exterior.

"Whatever," he replied, tossing his books into the back.

"Thanks." Stan slid into the empty seat and smiled as Mark followed the van from the school parking lot. They were driving in silence, but Stan knew he'd already said more to Mark than words could express.

Processing

In Jesus' day most Jews avoided contact with Samaritans who were thought to be unclean. Jesus was an unconventional Jew. Not only did he speak with a Samaritan, but he also spoke with a Samaritan *woman*. John 4 tells us Jesus knew the woman was living with a man she hadn't married, a sin for which her own peo-

DOWNLOAD BIBLE BYTE

When a Samaritan woman came to draw water, Jesus said to her, "Will you give me a drink?". . . The Samaritan woman said to him, "You are a Jew and I am a Samaritan woman. How can you ask me for a drink?"
John 4:7, 9

ple may have shunned her. Yet Jesus didn't hesitate to ask her for a drink of water and tell her about God.

While Jesus was speaking to the woman, the disciples had gone into town to buy food. When they returned, they were "surprised to find him talking with a woman" (John 4:27). Though the disciples respected Jesus enough to accept his behavior, others wouldn't have ignored his violation of Jewish custom. Jesus' reputation could have been permanently destroyed if other Jews had witnessed the exchange.

Do we reach out to "Samaritans" as Jesus did, without thought of jeopardizing our reputations? Or do we hide behind social customs, afraid to be seen as unclean? In Luke 5:31 Jesus said, "It is not the healthy who need a doctor, but the sick." As soon as Stan stepped into Mark's car, he risked being ridiculed by his friends. Stan's actions may have been unconventional, but they also showed that he was a follower of Jesus.

SAVING

Why did Jesus talk to the Samaritan woman?

Who are the Samaritans in your community?

How can you reach out to these people?

Facing the Hate

Joanne froze in her tracks when she spotted the graffiti painted across her locker. Every cuss word she'd ever heard of littered the tall metal door. Her eyes scanned the monstrosity, resting finally where someone had written "God" inside a circle with a line through it.

As she stood in the hallway staring at her defaced locker, Joanne felt sick to her stomach. *Maybe I should go to a Christian school,* she thought, imagining how much easier life would be among other believers. In a high school with fewer Christians than she had fingers, Joanne felt desperately alone. She'd refused to hide her relationship with God, always praying before meals and often talking about her faith in class discussions. *It's not like I'm hurting anybody,* she reasoned, struggling to understand why someone would do such a thing to her locker. *Why do they hate me?*

DOWNLOAD BIBLE BYTE

"If you belonged to the world, it would love you as its own. As it is, you do not belong to the world, but I have chosen you out of the world. That is why the world hates you."
John 15:19

Processing

Jesus knew better than anyone what it felt like to be hated by the world. He was insulted, beaten, mocked, and crucified because his life and teachings revealed the sin of humanity. Most of today's Christians escape such harsh persecution, but as Joanne discovered, Christians today still feel the world's hatred for God in a real way.

The world, which is "under the control of the evil one" (1 John 5:19), hates us because we are God's children. When we face the difficulties of being Christians in a lost world, it can be tempting to run and hide. Wouldn't life be better if we surrounded ourselves with people who understand us and believe as we do?

Jesus' prayer in John 17:15 shows us that leaving the world isn't the answer: "My prayer is not that you take them out of the world but that you protect them from the evil one." Christian schools can be helpful to many of us, and there's nothing wrong with attending one. But we have to be careful not to cut ourselves off from those who don't know God.

Regardless of where we go to school or what kind of persecution we face, we have a job to do—to spread God's message of love and salvation. Satan hates us because we're on God's side, and the devil will do everything possible to get in our way. But Romans 16:19–20 says, "Be wise about what is good, and innocent about what is evil. The God of peace will soon crush Satan under your feet."

HIGHLIGHT

The hatred we feel from the world can't compare to the love we have from God.

SAVING

When have you felt hated by the world?

Why does the world hate you?

How should we react to the world's hatred?

Misguided Boasting

Rich took the exam from his teacher's hand and peaked at the grade. Relief washed over him. Not only had he passed the midterm, he'd gotten a 96! Feeling a tap on his shoulder, Rich turned to the student behind him.

"How'd you do?" Bret asked. His giant grin told Rich he wasn't the only student with an A.

"Better than I thought I would," he replied.

"I got a 94," Bret said quickly, pride dripping from his voice. He craned his neck to look at the other students' papers. "I'll bet that's the highest grade!" Rich bit his tongue and read over the words of praise his teacher had written on the exam. He was itching to put Bret in his place by telling him about the 96.

As other students began filing their exams in their folders, Rich turned again to Bret. "Well?" Bret said. "Are you going to congratulate me, or what?"

Processing

When Daniel stood before Nebuchadnezzar, his life depended on his ability to describe and interpret the king's dream. Thankfully, God had revealed the dream and its meaning to Daniel. If he'd wanted to, Daniel could have shown his knowledge to the king and never mentioned God's intervention. But before Nebuchadnezzar could praise him as a wise man or magician, Daniel gave all the credit to God.

DOWNLOAD BIBLE BYTE

The king asked Daniel . . . , "Are you able to tell me what I saw in my dream and interpret it?" Daniel replied, "No wise man, enchanter, magician or diviner can explain to the king the mystery he has asked about, but there is a God in heaven who reveals mysteries."
Daniel 2:26–28

Most people wouldn't have behaved as Daniel did. Everyone wants praise, and that's why people like Bret and Rich feel the need to boast about their accomplishments. There's nothing wrong with wanting approval and applause, but there's only one thing we should boast about. Jeremiah 9:24 says, "Let him who boasts boast about this: that he understands and knows me, that I am the Lord, who exercises kindness, justice and righteousness on earth."

Daniel didn't have magical power that allowed him to read Nebuchadnezzar's mind or predict the future. He could do those things only because of God's power. The same was true of Rich, which is why it would be wrong for him to boast about his grade. "Every good and perfect gift is from above, coming down from the Father of the heavenly lights" (James 1:17). God enables us to be successful.

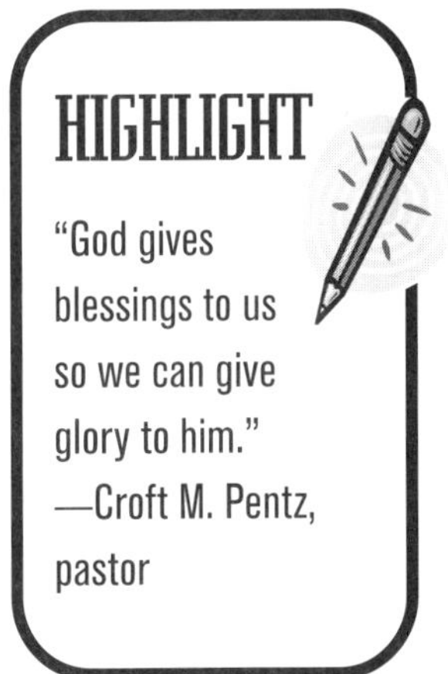

SAVING

For what do people praise you?

What is your typical response to being praised?

Why should we boast about God?

Clean Words from a Clean Heart

Sandra watched as Angie nursed her swollen knee during halftime. The field hockey game had been rough on everyone, but Angie's injury was the most severe. When an opponent had accidentally driven the ball into her leg, Angie had gone down with a cry of pain. *But she didn't swear,* Sandra remembered. *She never swears.*

Sandra didn't use much profanity either, but when she and her teammates were on the field, cussing seemed to come naturally. If the opposing team scored a goal or someone suffered an injury, swear words flowed freely from everyone. *Except Angie.*

"How's the knee, Ang?" Sandra asked as the referee blew her whistle. "Can you play?" Angie shook her head. "I'd better not," she said sadly, then grinned. "I'll just cheer you on from the sidelines." Sandra returned the smile and ran onto the field. There was something different about Angie, and Sandra was determined to find out what it was.

DOWNLOAD BIBLE BYTE

But among you there must not be . . . [any] obscenity, foolish talk or coarse joking, which are out of place, but rather thanksgiving.
Ephesians 5:3–4

Processing

A lot of people treat profanity like it's part of their natural vocabulary. Cuss words show up in all kinds of conversations. Sometimes they express frustration or pain, but often they're slipped into sentences without any apparent reason. The excess of profanity around us makes it difficult to keep our own minds and mouths clean. If profanity feels so natural, why is it wrong?

Our words reflect our values, beliefs, and personalities. Jesus once said, "For out of the overflow of the heart the mouth speaks" (Matthew 12:34). Profanity expresses negativity, anger, and dirty thoughts. When we speak profanity, what are we saying about our hearts? The verses from Ephesians remind us that we should be praising God rather than cursing the annoyances and difficulties in our lives.

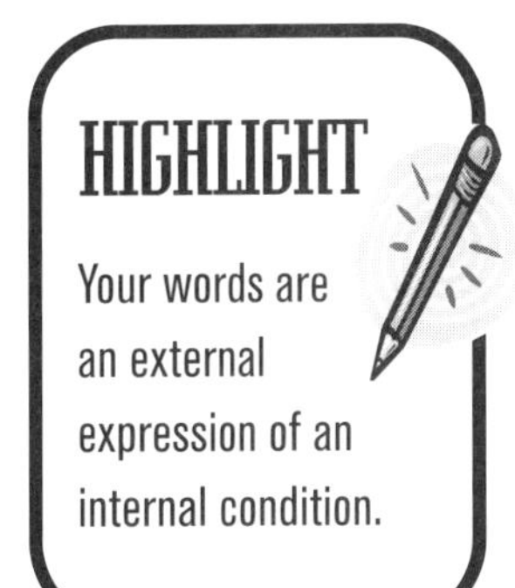

Clean language can also be an effective tool for talking to others about God. Think of how Angie's words affected Sandra. Profanity has become common in daily conversation. If we refrain from using it, people will notice. Our wholesome words will stand out from the filth around us, and eventually someone's bound to ask why we're different. The simple act of controlling our tongues can lead to opportunities to tell others about how God has changed our hearts.

SAVING

When is it most difficult to keep your language clean?

Why do people use profanity and laugh at dirty jokes?

For what should we use our words?

Outcast Company

Y*ikes! Not many seats left,* Sherry thought, standing at the front of the bus. The class trip to Florida would be a long one, so Sherry planned to choose her seat wisely.

She spotted an empty seat at the rear of the bus near Tammy. Tammy and Sherry had a lot in common. Besides going to the same church, they both played tennis, they liked the same music, and they were both on the honor roll. *I'll sit there,* Sherry thought, excited about the chance to talk with Tammy for hours.

On her way, though, Sherry noticed an empty seat beside Katrina. Nobody ever sat by Katrina because, as Sherry's friends put it, she was "weird." Even teachers looked at her with a raised eyebrow.

The girl glanced up at Sherry.

As Sherry walked between the seats, she argued with herself about what to do.

DOWNLOAD BIBLE BYTE

A man with leprosy came and knelt before him and said, "Lord, if you are willing, you can make me clean." Jesus reached out his hand and touched the man. "I am willing," he said. "Be clean!" Immediately he was cured of his leprosy.
Matthew 8:2–3

Processing

Lepers were outcasts in Jesus' day. According to Levitical law people with leprosy were unclean, which meant they were to be isolated from the rest of the community. They were required by law to cry out, "Unclean, unclean!" so that everyone would know to stay away from them. Nobody touched lepers in first-century Palestine.

Well, almost nobody. Jesus touched lepers. He stepped into the outcast's world and turned it upside down with love. With a single touch the leper was cured. Jesus did not stay away from the people that everyone else avoided. He pierced the social barrier. He loved the unlovely!

Leprosy is becoming increasingly rare, especially in the United States, but that doesn't mean outcasts are rare. If we're serious about following Jesus, we'll do two things. First, we'll make a promise to ourselves that if the opportunity presents itself, we'll step into the world of the outcasts around us. We won't allow ourselves to look the other direction. Second, we'll look for opportunities to make good on that promise.

> **HIGHLIGHT**
>
> "The biggest disease today is not leprosy or tuberculosis, but rather the feeling of being unwanted."
> —Mother Teresa

SAVING

Who are the outcasts around you?

What are some specific things you can do to show compassion for isolated people?

What are some possible rewards for serving outcasts?

Quarrel-Free Living

"God isn't actually *real*, you know," Drew grumbled as Nate walked by him. Nate's shoulders stiffened, and he stopped walking. Drew had pulled him into this argument before, and Nate didn't want to react the way he usually did, with anger and resentment.

"Yes he is, Drew," he said calmly.

Drew laughed. "I can't believe you're still buying into that Sunday school nonsense," he said. "Grow up, man." Nate took a deep breath, determined to respond kindly to Drew's challenges.

"Drew, just look around you. God exists. There's evidence of him everywhere."

"You can believe that lie if you want. I'm not going to be stupid."

"You're *not* stupid, Drew," Nate said calmly, meeting his cold gaze. "That's why I know you'll see the truth if you just open your eyes to it." Drew looked away then, but not quickly enough to hide the flicker of curiosity in his eyes.

DOWNLOAD BIBLE BYTE

"And [the Lord's servant must not quarrel; instead, he must be kind to everyone, able to teach, not resentful.

2 Timothy 2:24

Processing

The Bible Byte in this study was written to Timothy, who lived among the Christians in Ephesus. People in Timothy's church were divided by differing beliefs about "myths and endless genealogies" (1 Timothy 1:4). The apostle Paul referred to these arguments as "foolish and stupid" (2 Timothy 2:23), warning

Timothy to avoid them because they would produce quarrels.

Why was Paul against quarrels? Perhaps because he knew that they are seldom productive. More often than not, the end result of a quarrel is hurt feelings and not much else.

Religion has always been a source of debate and disagreement. No one enjoys having their beliefs challenged, and when people disagree with us, we tend to become defensive and argumentative. Sometimes our arguments are about major issues, but very often they are about unimportant details. Either way, we are told that quarreling is the wrong approach when speaking to others about Christianity. That doesn't mean we shouldn't state what we believe, but fighting is not the way to go.

If we're going to be "able to teach," we can't show resentment or anger toward those who question our beliefs. Colossians 3:14 tells us to "put on love" above all other virtues. As servants of the Lord, we should share his message with the same love he's shown us. When someone challenges your convictions, remember Paul's instruction to Timothy. Be kind, not resentful, and above all else, be loving.

HIGHLIGHT

"We are not won by arguments that we can analyze, but by tone and temper."
—Samuel Butler, English novelist

SAVING

Have you ever fought with someone about your religious beliefs? What was the result?

Why do you think Paul was against quarreling?

How should we respond when tempted to quarrel?

Shining from the Hilltops

Dan groaned as he sank into a chair. He'd been waiting tables for hours, and his feet were screaming for a rest.

"It's an awful job, isn't it?" Tina asked, watching him from across the room. Dan smiled and shook his head.

"It's tough, that's for sure. But it's nice to have a job." He was silent as he thought of his friends who hadn't found summer employment.

Tina rose from her chair and came to sit by Dan. Crushing the butt of her cigarette in an ashtray, she looked at him intently.

"Dan, I don't get you," she said, throwing up her hands. "I mean, you're not like anybody I know. You don't smoke. You don't cuss, even when you get stiffed on a tip. You never complain about anything, including this stupid job. What makes you so different?"

DOWNLOAD BIBLE BYTE

"You are the light of the world. A city on a hill cannot be hidden. . . . Let your light shine before men, that they may see your good deeds and praise your Father in heaven."
Matthew 5:14, 16

Processing

In Jesus' time cities were often built of white limestone. During the day their buildings gleamed in the sunlight and could be seen from far away. At night the cities were visible by the flames of the inhabitants' oil lamps. Jesus says if we follow him we should be like these ancient cities, shining brightly twenty-four hours a day.

Jesus said, "I am the light of the world. Whoever follows me will never walk in darkness, but will have the light of life" (John 8:12). We're the light of the world because Jesus was the light of the world. As his representatives, we have the responsibility of living as he did. Ephesians 5:8–9 tells us how to do that: "Live as children of light (for the fruit of the light consists in all goodness, righteousness and truth)."

Dan had never talked about Christianity, but Tina saw the "fruit of light" in his lifestyle. Our lights shine brighter through actions than words. People watch to see if we "practice what we preach." If we're constantly striving to live lives that are consistent with our beliefs, Jesus' light will shine through us. People will see by our actions that we're his followers, and our good deeds will bring praise to our Father in heaven.

HIGHLIGHT

"Setting an example is not the main means of influencing another, it is the only means."
—Albert Einstein

SAVING

How can you be the light of the world in your everyday life?

What did Tina notice about Dan?

Why do actions often speak louder than words?

Uncompromising Convictions

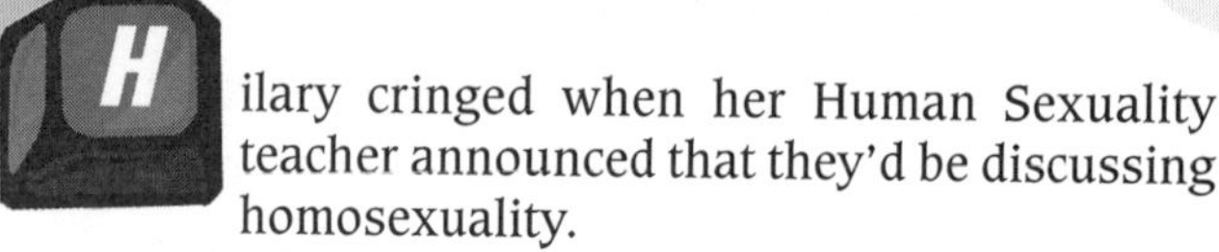

Hilary cringed when her Human Sexuality teacher announced that they'd be discussing homosexuality.

"First of all," the teacher said, "is there anyone here who thinks homosexuality is wrong?" The teacher's voice implied she expected the question to go unanswered. Hilary knew she was the only person in class with a conviction against homosexuality, but she hesitantly raised her hand.

"I do," she said, wishing she could disappear as all eyes turned toward her. Hilary's classmates didn't try to hide their contempt.

"Unbelievable," someone muttered from the corner. *This isn't going to be easy*, Hilary told herself, but she wasn't about to back down. Sitting up straight, Hilary looked at Mrs. Swanson. "I believe homosexuality is wrong."

Processing

When Shadrach, Meshach, and Abednego refused to bow to Nebuchadnezzar's idol, the king was furious. He warned the men that they'd be thrown into a fiery furnace unless they obeyed. Shadrach, Meshach, and Abednego refused once again, claiming their God would save them from death. When Nebuchadnezzar carried out his threat and saw the flames didn't even singe a hair on their heads, he praised God and rewarded the three men for their faith and courage.

DOWNLOAD BIBLE BYTE

Then Nebuchadnezzar said, "Praise be to the God of Shadrach, Meshach and Abednego. . . . They trusted in him and defied the king's command and were willing to give up their lives rather than serve or worship any god except their own God."
Daniel 3:28

Shadrach, Meshach, and Abednego refused to compromise. They could have bowed to the idol to spare their own lives, but they were willing to die before breaking God's commandment: "You shall not make for yourself an idol. . . .You shall not bow down to them or worship them" (Exodus 20:4–5). Most of us are not threatened with death because of our religious convictions, but do we show the same unwavering faith and conviction of Shadrach, Meshach, and Abednego?

In a world that lives by the motto "look out for Number One," the thought of willingly undergoing suffering seems radical. Nevertheless God expects nothing less than our absolute devotion. Sometimes that means standing firm in the midst of ridicule or persecution, like Hilary. It's tough to be firm, but like Shadrach, Meshach, and Abednego, our faithfulness will be rewarded.

HIGHLIGHT

"The ultimate measure of a man is not where he stands in moments of comfort and convenience, but where he stands at times of challenge and controversy."
—Martin Luther King Jr.

SAVING

What might have been the consequences of Hilary's statement?

When have you found yourself in a similar situation?

How can you stand firm for God in your life?

Breakable Vessels

Dale's anger swelled as Bill followed him across the parking lot. During gym class Dale had ducked to protect himself from Bill's line drive hit, and the boy had been mocking him ever since. "Maybe tomorrow you should join the girls," Bill taunted. "They're doing ballet."

Dale turned and punched Bill, knocking him to the ground. As Dale bent over him, Bill seized the opportunity to kick Dale in the face. Moments later two teachers came running to break up the scuffle.

Sitting outside the principal's office Dale nursed his swollen lip. "I'm sorry, Bill," he said to Bill, who glared at him from across the room. "I shouldn't have lost control." His words were sincere, but apologizing didn't make Dale feel any better. *What kind of example am I now?* he asked himself.

"I thought Christians weren't supposed to fight," Bill muttered. He tried to sound angry, but Dale's apology surprised him. Bill had provoked the fight and Dale had taken the bait, but there was still something beneath the surface that surprised Bill. He was beginning to think there might be something different about Dale after all.

DOWNLOAD BIBLE BYTE

But we have this treasure in jars of clay to show that this all-surpassing power is from God and not from us.
2 Corinthians 4:7

Processing

No doubt many of us have found ourselves in Dale's position. We do something sinful in front of people who know we're Christians, and they confront us about our actions. How are we supposed to respond when we're accused of being sinners in spite of our faith in God?

Well, we can start by agreeing with them. Christians are supposed to be different, but we're not *perfect*. We shouldn't use our imperfection as an excuse to sin, but we have to remember that we *are* sinful. In fact, according to Paul's illustration above, we're comparable to "jars of clay." Clay jars chip and break easily. They aren't worth a penny when it comes to standing up against pressure.

As usual, God turns bad into good. He uses our weakness to draw attention to his strength. When our jars of clay crack, his light shines through. Bill saw Dale's loving heart even though Dale messed up. As we persevere through difficulties, people will see the all-surpassing power inside us. By admitting to our own weaknesses, we can show people that God is the source of all the goodness and strength we possess.

SAVING

How are we like clay jars?

What are some of the cracks in your "clay jar"?

How should we respond to accusations about our sinfulness?

Wise Fools

The trial was over and television cameras swarmed around Robert as he faced his brother's murderer. The case had made national news and viewers wanted to see the teen's reaction to meeting the man who'd killed his brother.

Robert's body trembled at the coldness in the man's expression. *Isn't he supposed to feel remorse?* Robert wondered. *How can you ask me to forgive him, God?*

The room fell silent. Robert could almost hear people encouraging him to condemn the killer. *I'll look like a fool if I don't,* he realized, but once again he felt God tugging at his heart. *Forgive as I forgave you.*

Forgetting the cameras, Robert finally put his hand out and touched the man's arm. "I forgive you," he whispered. "Because God forgave me, I forgive you." The courtroom erupted with surprised murmurs, and the coldness in the man's expression changed to confusion. As Robert turned away, he noticed reporters staring at him as if he were crazy.

DOWNLOAD BIBLE BYTE

We have been made a spectacle to the whole universe. . . . We are fools for Christ . . . when we are cursed, we bless; when we are persecuted, we endure it; when we are slandered, we answer kindly.

1 Corinthians 4:9–10, 12–13

Processing

Devout Christians who are often among non-Christians know what it feels like to be "fools for Christ." If we're surrounded daily by people who don't understand our beliefs, stunned looks and surprised murmurs are part of the regular routine. We do things that contradict normal behavior, like loving when we're hated and forgiving when we're wronged. These things don't make sense to people who don't know God, so in their eyes we look like fools.

When people look at us like we're idiots, we have to remember whose approval we're seeking. Being fools for Christ is nothing to be ashamed about. If the world sees you as a fool for Christ, it means you're succeeding in obeying God. First Corinthians 1:20 and 25 say, "Has not God made foolish the wisdom of the world? . . . For the foolishness of God is wiser than man's wisdom."

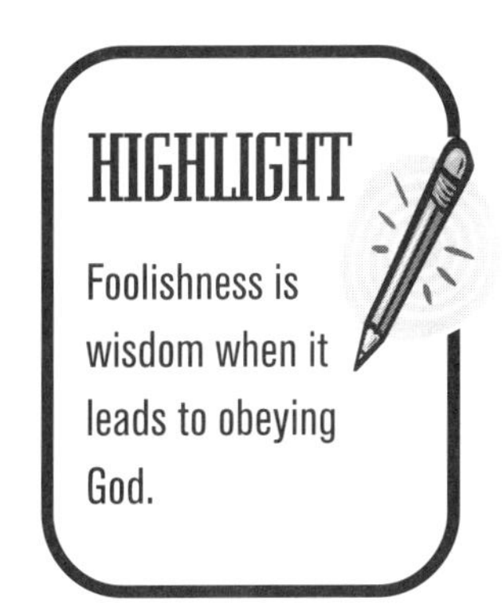

Remember that the Christian life is a life of standing out—our actions don't always seem to fit our circumstances. Consider Paul and Silas. When they were beaten and thrown into prison, they sat down and sang praises to God. They probably looked like fools to the other prisoners, but to God their songs were beautiful.

SAVING

What kinds of things make you feel like a fool for Christ?

Why shouldn't we be ashamed of godly foolishness?

How do you think the world's wisdom is foolish?

Restraining the Complaining

"Allen, mop the kitchen floors before you leave. The morning shift didn't do a good enough job." The two other dishwashers watched Allen for his reaction, expecting him to be angry.

"Okay," was all Allen said, though he wanted to complain. He was already an hour late getting off his shift, and it wasn't his fault the morning workers didn't do their jobs. But with everyone's eyes on him, Allen refused to protest.

His boss had been unfair before. It was something Allen would address in private, but he wasn't about to complain in front of everyone else. "Be different," his father had told him.

As soon as his boss walked away, one of the dishwashers nudged him. "Can you believe that guy? Doesn't he realize you're late already?" *My thoughts exactly*, Allen wanted to reply, but instead he looked on the bright side.

"Some extra work isn't going to kill me," he said. "Besides, I can use the money."

DOWNLOAD BIBLE BYTE

Be joyful always; pray continually; give thanks in all circumstances, for this is God's will for you in Christ Jesus. 1 Thessalonians 5:16

Processing

Life can be rough—full of pain, violence, and unfair suffering. When we're cheated, hurt, or saddled with unpleasant responsibilities, the natural course of action is to complain. Isn't that what everyone else does? If you sit and listen to the people around you, chances are you'll hear plenty of complaints from everyone.

Life isn't always a bed of roses, and all of us have problems we'd like to voice our opinions about. But according to Philippians 2:14–15, Christians are supposed to take a different approach to dealing with problems: "Do everything without complaining or arguing, so that you may become blameless and pure, children of God without fault in a crooked and depraved generation, in which you shine like stars in the universe." Do *everything* without complaining? Isn't that a little extreme?

Yes, it is extreme, but being extreme is the only way to show people we're different. The apostle Paul suggests that by refusing to speak negatively, we stand out amidst the grumbling of others. Over time people will notice the difference in us, and their curiosity will give us a chance to share about God. Being a Christian is about being radical, and sometimes that means we say "thank you, God," when someone else would say "woe is me."

HIGHLIGHT

"Some people are always grumbling because roses have thorns; I am thankful that thorns have roses."
—Alphonse Karr, French author

SAVING

What are some things we usually complain about?

What should we do instead of complaining?

What do Paul's words suggest about Allen's reaction to his boss?

Shelter in the Storm

"Would you like another blanket, Grandma?" Alissa asked.

"No, thank you, dear," her grandmother said. "Come sit with me." She patted the mattress. Alissa lifted herself onto the hospital bed and took her grandmother's wrinkled hand. It felt cold and stiff. Alissa looked away and focused on the monitors beside the bed.

"It won't be long now," her grandmother whispered, studying Alissa's strained expression.

"Are you scared, Grandma?" she asked.

"Not at all, honey," her grandmother replied. When Alissa didn't respond, she asked, "You don't believe me?"

"I don't understand. I know I'd be scared," Alissa replied.

"I have a safe passage," her grandmother explained. "God has been my shelter in life, and he'll be my shelter in death."

DOWNLOAD BIBLE BYTE

For forty days the flood kept coming on the earth, and as the waters increased they lifted the ark high above the earth. . . . Everything on dry land that had the breath of life in its nostrils died. . . . Only Noah was left, and those with him in the ark.

Genesis 7:17, 22–23

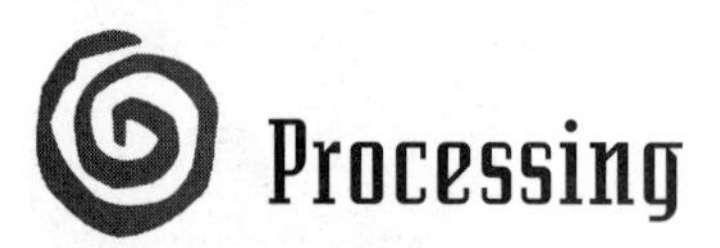

Processing

When the floodwaters came in Noah's day, the ark was the only escape from death. God chose to save Noah and his family because Noah was a righteous man. Everyone who had turned away from God perished because of their disobedience.

Noah and his family were on the ark for at least 150 days. They may have wondered whether God was going to make them float forever! But one day Noah's dove returned with an olive leaf, which meant the water had receded. Soon after, God told Noah and his family and all of the animals to come out. They were to begin life anew.

Just as the ark was the only shelter from the forty-day storm, God is our shelter from the crises we face. If we devote ourselves to him, nothing can destroy us. We may get tired of navigating the swells and breakers of life, but the waves will never overwhelm us when we depend on God. Eventually he will set us on dry land for a fresh start, either by blessing our obedience on earth or by giving us eternal life when we die.

HIGHLIGHT

No matter how hard the rains fall, we can always find warmth and safety in the shelter of God's love.

SAVING

Why wasn't Alissa's grandmother afraid of dying?

How is God a shelter?

What are some possible reasons God did not make the waters recede sooner?

Walking the Talk

As soon as the bus reached the lodge, Jen headed for the fireplace. She'd been skiing for hours with the youth group, and it was time to get some feeling back into her fingers and toes.

The lodge was crowded and only one empty chair remained by the fire. Jen was about to collapse into it when Randy Snyder bolted past her and sprawled across the chair.

"Sorry. Seat taken," he said, but his teasing grin told her he wasn't sorry at all.

"Please, Randy. I'm so cold," Jen pleaded, trying to keep her teeth from chattering.

"Oh well," he said, swinging his legs over the armrest. "You snooze, you lose."

Jen turned away and hunted for another chair. There was no point arguing with Randy. He was always trying to get under everyone's skin. Sometimes his behavior made Jen wonder if he was a Christian. *There's no way to know what's in his heart,* Jen thought, and then scolded herself for judging him. *But shouldn't a Christian act like a Christian?*

DOWNLOAD BIBLE BYTE

As the body without the spirit is dead, so faith without deeds is dead.

James 2:26

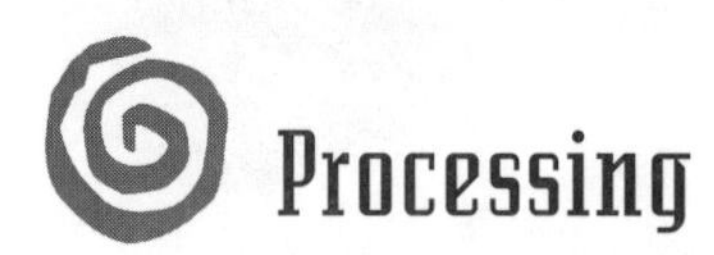

Processing

For years Bible scholars have struggled with James's teaching about faith and deeds. The verse above seems to imply that good works are necessary for salvation, yet the apostle Paul teaches that we can only be saved through faith in Christ. In Ephesians 2:8–9

Paul writes, "For it is by grace you have been saved, through faith—and this not from yourselves, it is the gift of God—not by works." Is James's teaching inconsistent with the teaching of Paul?

James's message isn't that good deeds are necessary for salvation, but that faith should affect a person's behavior. If someone has faith in Christ, their works should reflect the love Jesus showed during his life. That's why Randy's cruel behavior made Jen question his faith.

James uses the image of the body and spirit to illustrate the relationship between faith and deeds. Without the spirit, our bodies would be like zombies in a horror flick—wandering around without personality or emotion. Our spirits show that there's life inside us, and good works show that we have faith. Just like the body and the spirit together make a living person, faith and works should be inseparable in a living Christian.

HIGHLIGHT

If we've invited God into our hearts, evidence of his presence should flow through us, affecting our actions, words, and thoughts.

SAVING

How should a Christian's behavior differ from Randy's?

How are faith and works related in your own life?

What do you think it means to show Jesus' love today?

Seeing and Knowing God

The bell's ring interrupted Mrs. Loomis's lecture on the Roman Empire. "Okay, everybody," she said. "We'll finish Roman religion tomorrow."

"Great," Wes muttered sarcastically. The Romans' idol worship disgusted him, but his teacher acted like there was nothing wrong with worshiping false gods.

"What's the matter, Wes?" Simon asked. "Not crazy about the Romans?"

"How'd you guess?"

"I understand the Romans better than I understand you," Simon said, tapping his history book. "At least their gods could be seen and touched."

"Their gods were made of gold and rock," Wes said.

"Yeah, but they were *there*," Simon said. "They existed. What proof do you have that *your* god exists?"

DOWNLOAD BIBLE BYTE

For since the creation of the world God's invisible qualities—his eternal power and divine nature—have been clearly seen, being understood from what has been made, so that men are without excuse.
Romans 1:20

Processing

Simon's question is familiar to many of us. How do we defend our belief in God when we can't point to a physical sign of his existence? We don't have to be able to see things to know they're real. No one can see wind, yet does anyone doubt its existence? No one can point at or touch love, but has any sane person ever claimed love isn't real?

As we can't see wind or love, neither can we see God. Yet, as we believe in wind and love because of evidence that they exist, we can also believe in God because of evidence that he exists. According to Romans 1:20, creation is great evidence for God's existence. Everything God made speaks of his power and creativity. The creation's testimony, along with our faith in the unseen, enables us to believe in an invisible Creator.

Even if God's existence is obvious to people, many continue to question God's love and refuse to believe in Jesus Christ. These people are missing the most important element of Christianity: faith. Hebrews 11:1 says, "Now faith is being sure of what we hope for and certain of what we do not see." Knowing God (as opposed to just admitting he exists) comes from a decision to have faith in him—to put one's own life in his hands. Christians are people who first believe in the evidence of God's existence and then take the extra step of placing their lives in God's loving hands.

HIGHLIGHT

"Understanding is the reward of faith. Therefore seek not to understand that thou mayest believe, but believe that thou mayest understand."
—Saint Augustine

SAVING

How do you answer someone who questions God's existence?

What are some things people believe by faith?

Why is faith so important to Christianity?

Separate or Alike?

Evan shoved his way through the mosh pit, desperate to escape the frenzied throng of rock fans. His head pounded from the screaming listeners and screeching guitars as he made his way back to his seat.

"Pretty cool, huh?" one of his friends yelled.

"Yeah," he yelled back, grabbing his water.

The lead singer ran back and forth across the stage, belting out Christian lyrics, while the bass guitarist peered down at his instrument through his curly black hair. The drummer's arms were everywhere, as the lead guitarist picked up the melody and took it to the stratosphere.

Evan couldn't help but compare this band to non-Christian bands he'd seen. *There's not much of a difference,* he thought. *I wonder if this music would bring my non-Christian friends closer to God.*

DOWNLOAD BIBLE BYTE

For what do righteousness and wickedness have in common? Or what fellowship can light have with darkness? What harmony is there between Christ and [Satan]? What does a believer have in common with an unbeliever?
2 Corinthians 6:14–15

Processing

Well-meaning, reasonable Christians differ about how separate we should be from non-Christians. Paul wrote, "I have become all things to all men so that by all possible means I might save some" (1 Corinthians 9:22). Some Christians hope they will gain a hearing from non-Christians by becoming like them.

Jesus spent time talking and dining with sinners, but never became like them, so other Christians say believers are to be very different from non-Christians.

They say non-Christians will be attracted to the difference.

In any case we should draw non-Christians to Christ. Matthew 5:16 says, "Let your light shine before men, that they may see your good deeds and praise your Father in heaven." When Evan went to the rock concert, he was forced to think about how separate or alike Christians should be to non-Christians. It is important for Christians to seek God's guidance in determining in their own hearts the best way to draw non-Christians to the gospel.

HIGHLIGHT

Drawing non-Christians to Christ is important business. It deserves your thought.

SAVING

What drew you to Christ?

What would you do if you were in a situation similar to Evan's?

How can you seek God's guidance in determining how you should live to draw others to Christ?

Worldwide Witnesses

"Did you know Henry before he became a missionary," Jared asked his father.

"We went to school together," he replied. "It was good to hear him give an update in church yesterday."

"How old was he was when he left for Africa?" Jared asked.

"Twenty-six, I think," his father said. "Why do you ask?"

"Listening to him made me excited about missions. I just wish I could get involved right away."

"What makes you think you can't?" his father asked. Jared laughed.

"Well, I'm still in high school for one thing," he said. "Being a missionary seems impossible right now."

"Maybe you can't work in Africa like Henry does," his father said, "but you don't have to leave the country to tell people about God."

DOWNLOAD BIBLE BYTE

"But you will receive power when the Holy Spirit comes on you; and you will be my witnesses in Jerusalem, and in all Judea and Samaria, and to the ends of the earth."
Acts 1:8

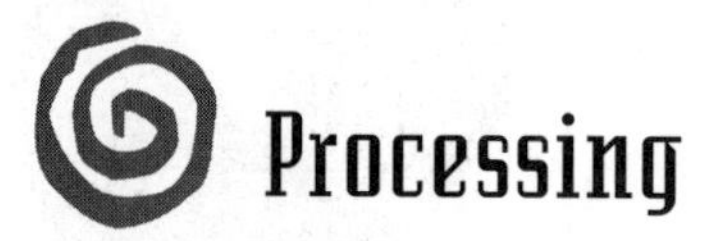

Processing

The words of Acts 1:8 were Jesus' last words to the disciples before he ascended into heaven. We often hear this command in reference to missionary work in foreign lands, but we don't have to be missionaries to tell people about God. Faraway countries are only part of the picture. Jesus also commanded the first-century Christians to be his witnesses at home, in Jerusalem, Judea, and Samaria.

Jerusalem was familiar territory to the disciples. They knew the city, the customs, and many of the people. Jesus wants us to share his message in our hometowns with our friends and neighbors. Judea and Samaria included the areas surrounding Jerusalem. The disciples may not have had as many personal connections throughout the region, but they still understood the people and their ways. Judea and Samaria to us might include surrounding states or other countries that are similar to our own.

Being a "witness" is about bringing the news of Jesus to people who don't know him, regardless of how geographically close or distant they are. Location isn't a requirement for sharing the good news. Jared was wrong to think he had to travel overseas to obey Jesus' command. If a person doesn't know him, it doesn't matter where they live. Our job is to reach as many lost people as possible in the time we've been given, whether they're on American soil or thousands of miles away.

HIGHLIGHT

In your quest to reach the lost man in India, don't overlook the lost man across the street.

SAVING

Who is someone in your "Jerusalem" that you can be a witness to?

Where do you feel God has called you to be his witness?

What do you think is the most important consideration in witnessing?

Timing Is Everything

"I don't share your religious beliefs, Gary, but many students do," Principal Nelson said. "I've been asked to find someone to lead a Bible study group at the school." Gary's eyes grew large at the principal's words. "I've surprised you?" Principal Nelson asked.

"Of course," Gary finally said. "I've been waiting to hear you say that for two years. I'd almost given up asking."

"Well, now I've asked," the principal said. "So are you interested, or should I find someone else?"

"I'd be happy to help," Gary said.

"Fine. I'll be in touch."

Gary rose to leave, but paused at the doorway. "Why now, instead of two years ago?" he asked. Principal Nelson shrugged.

"Maybe your God didn't have it on his agenda two years ago."

Gary smiled as he considered the man's words. "You may be more right than you realize."

DOWNLOAD BIBLE BYTE

Paul and his companions traveled throughout the region of Phrygia and Galatia, having been kept by the Holy Spirit from preaching the word in the province of Asia.
Acts 16:6

Processing

The apostle Paul traveled through the ancient world preaching about Jesus Christ. Paul wanted to go to Asia, but the Holy Spirit directed him elsewhere. Later, Paul finally entered Asia, preached the gospel, and many people put their faith in Jesus (Acts 19). Why didn't God allow Paul to preach in Asia to begin with?

God planned for Paul to go to Asia, but not when Paul originally wanted to. There could've been many reasons God prevented Paul from entering Asia. Perhaps the Asian people weren't ready to hear about Jesus. Perhaps there were others in Phrygia or Galatia who needed to hear the gospel right away. Whatever the reason for God's plan, Paul chose to obey, and as a result many people believed in Christ.

Ecclesiastes 3:11 says, "He has made everything beautiful in its time." God can see the past, present, and the future. He exists above time, so his schedule for our lives is perfect. Sometimes we can't understand why God closes doors on our plans, especially when we think our plans are pleasing to him. Paul may have felt the same way, wondering why God would prevent people in Asia from hearing about Jesus. But like Paul, we have to believe God's timing is perfect. When he closes a door, he may be giving a permanent answer or simply putting our plans on hold until a better time.

HIGHLIGHT

When God closes a door, he doesn't necessarily lock it and throw away the key.

SAVING

When have you questioned God's plans as Gary did?

What did Paul do instead of questioning God?

What are some reasons God might put your plans on hold?

Hiding under a Bowl

Mariah turned to look out the window as her bus passed Calvary Christian School. Teenage boys and girls stood by the road in clusters talking with their friends, and Mariah studied them curiously.

Mariah attended the public school, but she always wondered what life was like at the Christian school. She lived near many of Calvary's students, but she never spoke with them or saw them around town. The Christians belonged to a different world. Posters outside their school advertised concerts by bands Mariah had never seen. The church programs allowed the Christian teens to spend time together on weekends.

I wonder what they're really like, Mariah thought. She couldn't imagine those teens thinking about the same things she thought about, or struggling with the same issues she struggled with. *We probably have nothing in common.*

Processing

Christians today have created a subculture. We have our own schools, music, books, and movies. By surrounding ourselves with Christians and "Christian" products, many of us hope to protect ourselves from the temptations of popular society. But when we shut ourselves off from the real world, we put a bowl over the lamp of God's love.

DOWNLOAD BIBLE BYTE

"People [do not] light a lamp and put it under a bowl. Instead they put it on its stand, and it gives light to everyone in the house. In the same way, let your light shine before men, that they may see your good deeds and praise your Father in heaven."
Matthew 5:15–16

Living only among other Christians makes us feel comfortable and safe, but it isn't pleasing to God. While he wants us to have fellowship with believers, God also wants us to live as Jesus lived. Jesus didn't spend every moment with his disciples. He went into the world and taught about God through his words and actions. Jesus let his light shine even when he knew his boldness would bring neither comfort nor safety.

Of course, our Christian subculture offers many benefits. We have inspiring music, enlightening books, and first-rate educators. Christian institutions aren't a problem as long as we realize the importance of sharing God with the world. Jesus said, "It is not the healthy who need a doctor, but the sick" (Matthew 9:12). When we hide from the world, we keep God to ourselves. People need to learn about him, so let your light shine brightly as you follow in Jesus' steps.

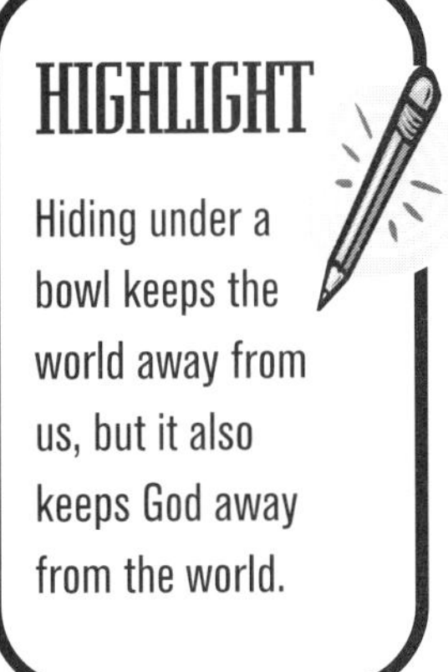

HIGHLIGHT

Hiding under a bowl keeps the world away from us, but it also keeps God away from the world.

SAVING

Do you spend most of your time inside or outside the Christian subculture?

Why is it wrong to cut ourselves off from the world?

How can we follow in Jesus' footsteps?

The Bible Bytes Finder

The Bible Bytes Finder makes it easy to locate any Bible Byte. Whether you want information about a particular passage or you're looking for the exact wording of a Bible Byte, here are Scripture references and page numbers for all the Bible Bytes in this book.

OLD TESTAMENT

Philippians

Colossians

1 Thessalonians

1 Timothy

2 Timothy

Hebrews

James

1 Peter

1 John

Subject Index

I

J

K

L

M

V

W

POPULAR BOOKS BY STARBURST PUBLISHERS®

Bible Bytes for Teens: A Study-Devotional for Logging In to God's Word
From the Creators of the God's Word for the Biblically-Inept™ *Series*
Growing up isn't easy in today's fast-paced world of e-this and i-that. Now, teens can exit off the information superhighway with a bit of the Bible. Each two-page lesson starts with an anecdote about an issue relevant to teens, includes a Bible verse, easy-to-understand devotional lesson, questions for application, and a power-packed takeaway.
(trade paper) ISBN 1892016494 **$12.95**

Bible Seeds: A Simple Study-Devotional for Growing in God's Word
From the Creators of the God's Word for the Biblically-Inept™ *Series*
Growing your faith is like tending a garden—just plant the seed of God's Word in your heart, tend it with prayer, and watch it blossom. At the heart of this unique study is a Bible verse or "seed" that is combined with an inspirational lesson, a word study, application tips, thought questions with room to write, a prayer starter, and a final thought.
(trade paper) ISBN 1892016443 **$12.95**

The *What's in the Bible for . . .*™ series focuses its attention on making the Bible applicable to everyday life. Whether you're a teenager or senior citizen, this series has the book for you! Each title is equipped with the same reader-friendly icons, call-outs, tables, illustrations, questions, and chapter summaries that are used in the *God's Word for the Biblically-Inept*™ series. It's another easy way to access God's Word!

What's in the Bible for . . .™ Teens
By Mark Littleton and Jeanette Gardner Littleton
The Bible may have been written a long time ago, but it is packed with help for today's teens. From peer pressure and parents to drugs and driving, this book addresses the rocky issues gripping today's youth and provides biblical insight with examples of teens in the Bible. Helpful WWJD icons, illustrations, chapter summaries, study questions, and commentary from contemporary musicians will capture the attention of readers and get them excited about a renewed relationship with God.
(trade paper) ISBN 1892016052 **$16.95**

What's in the Bible for . . .™ Mothers
By Judy Bodmer
Is home schooling a good idea? Is it okay to work? At what age should I start treating my children like responsible adults? What is the most important thing I can teach my children? If

you are asking these questions and need help answering them, *What's in the Bible for . . .*™ *Mothers* is especially for you! Simple and user-friendly, this motherhood manual offers hope and instruction for today's mothers by jumping into the lives of mothers in the Bible (e.g., Naomi, Elizabeth, and Mary) and by exploring biblical principles that are essential to being a nurturing mother.
(trade paper) ISBN 1892016265 **$16.95**

What's in the Bible for . . .*™ *Women
By Georgia Curtis Ling
What does the Bible have to say to women? Women of all ages will find biblical insight on topics that are meaningful to them in four sections: Wisdom for the Journey; Family Ties; Bread, Breadwinners, and Bread Makers; and Fellowship and Community Involvement. This book uses illustrations, bullet points, chapter summaries, and icons to make understanding God's Word easier than ever!
(trade paper) ISBN 1892016109 **$16.95**

• Learn more at www.learntheword.com •

God Stories: They're So Amazing, Only God Could Make Them Happen
By Donna I. Douglas
Famous individuals share their personal, true-life experiences with God in this beautiful book! Find out how God has touched the lives of top recording artists, professional athletes, and other newsmakers like Jessi Colter, Deana Carter, Ben Vereen, Stephanie Zimbalist, Cindy Morgan, Sheila E., Joe Jacoby, Cheryl Landon, Brett Butler, Clifton Taulbert, Babbie Mason, Michael Medved, Sandi Patty, Charlie Daniels, and more! Their stories are intimate, poignant, and sure to inspire and motivate you as you listen for God's message in your own life!
(cloth) ISBN 1892016117 **$18.95**

Halloween and Satanism
By Phil Phillips and Joan Hake Robie
This book traces the origins of Halloween and gives the true meaning behind this celebration of "fun and games." Jack-o'-lanterns, cats, bats, and ghosts are much more than costumes and window decorations. In this book you will discover that involvement in any form of the occult will bring you more than "good fortune." It will lead you deeper and deeper into the Satanic realm, which ultimately leads to death.
(trade paper) ISBN 091498411X **$9.95**

Purchasing Information
www.starburstpublishers.com

Books are available from your favorite bookstore, either from current stock or special order. To assist bookstores in locating your selection, be sure to give title, author, and ISBN. If unable to purchase from a bookstore, you may order direct from STARBURST PUBLISHERS. When ordering please enclose full payment plus shipping and handling as follows:

Post Office (4th class)
$4.00 with purchase of up to $20.00
$5.00 ($20.01–$50.00)
8% of purchase price for purchases of $50.01 and up

United Parcel Service (UPS)
$5.00 (up to $20.00)
$7.00 ($20.01–$50.00)
12 % ($50.01 and up)

Canada
$5.00 (up to $35.00)
15% ($35.01 and up)

Overseas
$5.00 (up to $25.00)
20% ($25.01 and up)

Payment in U.S. funds only. Please allow two to four weeks minimum for delivery by USPS (longer for overseas and Canada). Allow two to seven working days for delivery by UPS. Make checks payable to and mail to:

Starburst Publishers®
P.O. Box 4123
Lancaster, PA 17604

Credit card orders may be placed by calling 1-800-441-1456, Mon.–Fri., 8:30 A.M. to 5:30 P.M. Eastern Standard Time. Prices are subject to change without notice. Catalogs are available for a 9 X 12 self-addressed envelope with four first-class stamps.